Forgotten Black Soldiers Who Served in White Regiments During the Civil War

Revised Edition

Juanita Patience Moss

HERITAGE BOOKS
2008

HERITAGE BOOKS
AN IMPRINT OF HERITAGE BOOKS, INC.

Books, CDs, and more—Worldwide

For our listing of thousands of titles see our website
at
www.HeritageBooks.com

Published 2008 by
HERITAGE BOOKS, INC.
Publishing Division
100 Railroad Ave. #104
Westminster, Maryland 21157

Other books by the author:

Anthracite Coal Art of Charles Edgar Patience

Battle of Plymouth, North Carolina (April 17-20, 1864): The Last Confederate Victory

Created to Be Free: A Historical Novel about One American Family

The Forgotten Black Soldiers in White Regiments During the Civil War

International Standard Book Numbers
Paperbound: 978-0-7884-4647-4
Clothbound: 978-0-7884-7285-5

THIS BOOK IS DEDICATED TO THE MEMORY
OF
CROWDER PATIENCE (PACIEN)

(1848-1930)
PRIVATE COMPANY C
103RD PENNSYLVANIA VOLUNTEERS

P. | 103 | Pa.

Crowder Pacien

Appears with rank of Coll'd Cook on

Muster and Descriptive Roll of a Detachment of U. S. Vols. forwarded

for the 103 Reg't Pa. Infantry. Roll dated

Plymouth, N.C., Apr. 4, 1864.

Where born Chowan Co. N.C.

Age 18 y'rs; occupation Laborer

When enlisted Jan. 1, 1864.

Where enlisted Plymouth N.C.

For what period enlisted 3 years.

Eyes Black; hair Black

Complexion Black; height 5 ft. 5 in.

When mustered in Apr. 4, 1864.

Where mustered in Plymouth N.C.

Bounty paid $ 100; due $ 100

Where credited

Company to which assigned C.

Remarks: Enlisted in accordance with G.O. 73. Act 7. Sec. 10. series 1863 from War Dept.

Book mark:

Enlistment Record of Crowder Pacien

TABLE OF CONTENTS

"Once let the black man get upon his person the brass letters, **U.S.**, let him get an eagle on his button, and a musket on his shoulder and bullets in his pocket, and there is no power on earth which can deny that he has earned the right to citizenship in the United States."

Frederick Douglass

PHOTOGRAPHS AND DOCUMENTS

CERTIFICATE IN LIEU OF LOST OR DESTROYED

DISCHARGE CERTIFICATE.

PLURIBUS UNUM

To all Whom it May Concern:

Know ye, That Crowder Pacien a Private of Company C, One hundred and third Regiment of Pennsylvania Infantry VOLUNTEERS, who was enrolled on the first day of January, one thousand eight hundred and sixty-four, to serve three years was Discharged from the service of the United States on the twenty-fifth day of June, one thousand eight hundred and sixty-five, by reason of muster out of company.

This Certificate is given under the provisions of the Act of Congress approved July 1, 1902, "to authorize the Secretary of War to furnish certificates in lieu of lost or destroyed discharges," to honorably discharged officers or enlisted men or their widows, upon evidence that the original discharge certificate has been lost or destroyed, and upon the condition imposed by said Act that this certificate "shall not be accepted as a voucher for the payment of any claim against the United States for pay, bounty, or other allowances, or as evidence in any other case."

Given at the War Department, Washington, D. C., this fourth day of June, one thousand nine hundred and twelve.

By authority of the Secretary of War:

J. C. [illegible]

Adjutant General.

(A. G. O. 180)

Crowder Patience's Discharge Record

ACKNOWLEDGEMENTS

A number of experts aided me with this project. First, I acknowledge the valuable advice and knowledge received from Dr. Harold Cox, Professor of History Emeritus and University Archivist of Wilkes University, Wilkes Barre, Pennsylvania. After I sought his advice, he encouraged me to thoroughly research this topic that no one has before.

When I went to the State Library in Raleigh, North Carolina, to seek information from librarian Pam Toms, I discovered Broadfoot's thirty volumes of the ***Roster of Union Soldiers 1861-1865*** that would prove invaluable to my research. Of course, the first name I looked for was Private Crowder Pacien, locating his name easily in one of the Pennsylvania volumes.

At the Military Barracks at Carlisle, Pennsylvania, I was aided by Dr. Charles Summers. I also spent many hours at the Fairfax Library in Fairfax, Virginia, where librarian Susan Levy led me to additional information.

At the National Archives in Washington, D.C., Dennis Edelin and Lynn Nashorn were of great help with researching individual black soldiers' military records, as well as Acquisitions Librarian Torin C. Pollock who directed me to Union regimental histories.

I must mention Dr. Frank Smith, founding director of the African American Civil War Museum in Washington, D.C. His life-long dream had been to have a visual memorial created to honor the United States Colored Troops (USCT), and to that end he worked diligently until his goal was reached in 1998.

Dr. Smith was the first person I approached following a symposium on 15 July 1998, at which time I was told there had been no black soldiers in white regiments during the Civil War. Recognizing and respecting my zeal to prove otherwise, he has been quite encouraging throughout these past ten years.

I also thank Hari Jones, curator of the Museum, for his interest in my quest to discover the black soldiers whose names are not engraved on the wall surrounding the monument on U Street. Most recently, I owe thanks to historians Bennie McRae, Jr., Glenda McWither Todd, and Peggy Sawyer-Williams for the additional information they have provided for this revised and updated publication.

I, too, have a dream. It is to have a visual memorial created to remember the black soldiers who served in white regiments during the Civil War. They have been forgotten. They are "invisible men" whose names are "hidden in plain sight" within Union military records. This book is the first step towards achieving that goal.

As with my previous books, I must thank my friend and former colleague from Bloomfield High School, Bloomfield, New Jersey, Dr. June Bohannon-Powell, retired Chairperson of the Language Department, for her expert editing of my work. Of course, I must also acknowledge the continued interest and support of my publisher, Craig Scott of Heritage Books.

And most especially I am grateful to Edward Moss, my husband of almost fifty-six years. He is to be commended for his unflagging support and patience since I became obsessed with this project and addicted to my computer. Lastly, my heartfelt thanks to family and friends, far too numerable to mention by name, who have offered me encouragement and support in many ways.

Juanita Patience Moss
Alexandria, Virginia

PREFACE

Readers may wonder why I have used the word "forgotten" in regards to the black soldiers who served in white regiments during the Civil War. Why and how did those men become "forgotten?"

One very plausible explanation is that many of them lost track of their discharge records after receiving them. My great grandfather, for instance, first had to get a replacement in order to apply for a pension. Following the war, he lost the original during his travels. Most likely, through the G.A.R. (Grand Army of the Republic), in which he was a member he was able to obtain the necessary information, since he did receive a monthly pension until his death in 1930. The G.A.R. was the veterans' fraternal organization formed after the end of the war.

Other black veterans simply had no interest in remembering the bitter days prior to or during the war. They just wanted to relish their new lives as free men. Also many of their children did not want to know anything about their parents' lives when they had been slaves. Consequently, the participation of many of the black soldiers during the Civil War was not discussed and so, was not passed on to become family legacies. For instance, three generations of my family were to have come and gone before interest in the Civil War black soldiers would develop. The generations of my great grandfather Crowder, my grandfather Harry, and my father Charles Edgar Patience.

Many students in the United States have studied the Civil War in their history classes. However, not until the movie "Glory" was produced in 1989, did the black soldiers become of interest to the general public. Few history books contain any such information, even though several scholars have researched and published books about those particular soldiers.

The 166 regiments of the United States Colored Troops (USCT) had never been discussed in any of the history courses I ever took either in high school or in college. Certainly I studied certain aspects of the Civil War, such as learning important dates, decisive battles, and the names of leaders on both sides. At one time I could even recite Lincoln's Gettysburg Address because it was a requirement in one of my high school history classes. Never did I read anything about the participation of black soldiers, though.

Certainly, if I had grown up in the Boston, Massachusetts, area instead of northeastern Pennsylvania, I might have known about the 54th Massachusetts Infantry because of the bronze memorial that stands on the Boston Common. Created by Augustus Saint-Gaudens, it was dedicated on 28 May 1897 in memory of that valiant regiment of black men.

So, seeing "Glory" was my first step towards writing this book, even though I had no idea at the time that I would be researching and writing about black Civil War soldiers ten years later. The second step was the viewing of the eleven-foot bronze monument, "Spirit of Freedom," created in Washington, D.C., in 1998 to honor black soldiers and sailors who had served during the Civil War.

The third step was learning the reason for my great grandfather's name not being engraved on the encircling monument wall displaying the names of other black soldiers, even though I knew he had been a Civil War veteran. The reason being is that he had served in a white regiment.

The fourth step during these past ten years has been the collecting of as many names as I can find of other forgotten black soldiers who had served in white regiments during the Civil War, and not in the segregated ones. Now they, too, are finally being remembered.

CHAPTER I

United States Army Before the Civil War

Following the American Revolution, American ground forces had encountered only two foreign enemies on North American soil and had otherwise been limited to garrison duty and the pacification of Native Americans. In 1860 before the Civil War began, there had been 27,968 men serving in the American military, of which 16,215 were in the Army. A year later, the Army had increased more than twelve-fold to 186,845. The growth continued, and at the end of the war there were 1,000,692 soldiers in the Union Army, roughly eight percent of the entire male population of the country. [1]

The long bitter Civil War fought on American soil between 1861 and 1865 has been called by many names: The War Between the States, The War Against Northern Aggression, The Second American Revolution, The Lost Cause, The War For Southern Independence, and The War of the Rebellion. Regardless by what name it was called, that war was *"the most horrible, necessary, intimate, acrimonious, mean-spirited, and heroic conflict the nation has known."*[2] Having commenced as a dispute over national versus state sovereignty, it terminated as a struggle over the meaning of freedom for all persons living in America.

Such a rapid growth in the number of soldiers, combined with the need to maintain an industrial/ agricultural infrastructure adequate to support the military effort, placed a severe strain on manpower resources. Therefore, various incentives were offered to encourage volunteers, and a draft was instituted. Even though the Union needed to increase the declining numbers of white volunteers, free blacks were not encouraged to enlist; in fact, the exact opposite was true.

Shortly after the war had erupted, many free blacks in the North made the attempt to join the Union Army, but were flatly rejected since President Abraham Lincoln believed their conscription would further alienate northern whites and the loyal border-states of Delaware, Kentucky, Maryland, and Missouri. He could ill afford that and, also, he believed that the "Negro problem" could be solved by re-colonizing blacks elsewhere.

As early as 1861, Radical Republicans and abolitionists, such as the outspoken black orator Frederick Douglass, tried to persuade Lincoln to allow free blacks to enlist as soldiers. Lincoln's adamant denial caused abolitionists to wonder if they had made a disastrous mistake in supporting Abraham Lincoln for president.(3) A situation they considered very disturbing was the Administration's vacillating policy toward the "colored refugees," those runaways fleeing southern plantations to seek the protection of the Federal troops who, even though they had no love for slavery, had no love either for the slaves.

The Republicans and abolitionists also requested that a policy be created concerning those fugitive slaves. The Republicans and abolitionists demanded a set government policy be established concerning both the fugitives and their emancipation. Since no policy had been established by the Administration, each commander was using his own discretion toward the refugees.(4)

As such an example, upon learning in May of 1861 that slaves in Virginia were being used to erect Confederate defenses, General Benjamin Butler issued the order that three escaping blacks not be returned to their owner when he came under a flag of truce behind the Yankee line to claim his property. Instead, Butler rationalized that the blacks were Confederate property, or "contrabands of war," e.g. possessions to be awarded to the victor. Unwilling to return them to their masters, but unable legally to free them, he put them to work for the Union Army at Fort Monroe, Virginia.(5)

Three months later the Confiscation Act of August 6, 1861 was issued by the Government. It stated that any property used in insurrection against the United States was to be taken as contraband, and when that property was slaves, they were "forever free." [6]

Other generals reacted in several differing ways towards the fugitives. In Missouri, a border-state not in insurrection, General John C. Fremont issued an order on 30 August 1861 to confiscate all Confederate property, including slaves, who were then to be considered free. However, based upon the terms of the Confiscation Act, President Lincoln disavowed Fremont's premature order of emancipation for the slaves and, consequently, on 2 October 1861 General Fremont was relieved of his command. [7]

Seeking the protection of the Union Army that would guarantee their freedom, fleeing contrabands became overcrowded in lamentable disease-ridden camps. To help alleviate the problem, General Ulysses Simpson Grant in 1862 appointed sympathetic army officers to supervise the utilization of the services of all fugitive slaves behind his lines in western Tennessee, [8] the same policy subsequently developing in many other occupied areas.

The contrabands were used for military support, such as cooks and undercooks. Then after the Emancipation Proclamation was signed on 1 January 1863, many enlisted in the Union Army. This book contains the names of hundreds of those particular soldiers, whose names are not difficult to find due to General Orders 323 that allowed blacks to enlist as undercooks in white regiments of the Union Army.

GENERAL ORDERS No. 323. [9]

WAR DEPT., *ADJT. GENERAL'S OFFICE*

Washington, September 28, 1863.

In section 10, act of March 3, 1863, it is enacted "That the President of the United States be, and he is hereby, authorized to cause to be enlisted for each cook (two allowed by section 9) two undercooks of African descent, who shall receive for their full compensation $10 per month and one ration per day; $3 of said monthly pay may be in clothing.

For a regular company, the two undercooks will be enlisted; for a volunteer company, they will be mustered into service, as in the cases of other soldiers. In each case a remark will be made on their enlistment papers showing that they are undercooks of African descent. Their names will be borne on the company muster-rolls at the foot of the list of privates. They will be paid, and their accounts will be kept, like other enlisted men. They will also be discharged in the same manner as other soldiers.

By order of the Secretary of War:

E.D. TOWNSEND,

Assistant Adjutant-General

CHAPTER II

Black Men and the Union Army

In spite of President Lincoln's initial objections, several units of black men were formed, such as General Benjamin Butler's *Corps d'Afrique.* Originally raised to serve the Confederacy, the Louisiana Native Guards were mainly free men of mixed ancestry. They were men who identified with the white population rather than with the black. They were men of property, some themselves slave owners. Even so, they never were mustered into the Confederate Army. Finally they absorbed the bitter fact that they would never be given the same respect accorded the white soldiers.

After the fall of New Orleans on 29 April 1862, due to their military experience General Butler recruited approximately 1,000 members of the *Corps d'Afrique* to become Union soldiers organized into two regiments staffed entirely by black officers, including Major F. E. Dumas and Captain P. B. S. Pinchback.[(10)] Subsequently, the 1st Regiment of the Louisiana Native Guards was sworn into the Union Army on 27 September 1862 with the 2nd and 3rd Regiments following in October and November. These three regiments had the distinction of being the first black units officially mustered into the Union Army.

Later, in August 1862 the 1st Kansas Colored Infantry Regiment was organized, consisting primarily of fugitive slaves from Arkansas and Missouri. Originally under the direction of a general in the state militia, abolitionist Senator James Lane, the 1st Kansas later would be led by Colonel James M. Williams.

This unofficial regiment was in defiance of the policies in the Confiscation Act set by President Abraham Lincoln and Secretary of War Edwin Stanton. Regardless, on 29 October 1862 the 1st Kansas Colored Infantry skirmished with a unit of Rebel guerrillas at Island Mound, Missouri, thereby giving it the distinction of being the first black unit to engage the enemy. This action occurred even before the regiment, being the fourth black one, was mustered into Federal service on 13 January 1863 as the 79th USCI (United States Colored Infantry).[11]

Months before on 9 May 1862 at Hilton Head, S. C., Major General David Hunter, Commander of the Department of the South, had issued an "emancipation proclamation" of his own, intending to grant freedom to all slaves in Florida, Georgia, and South Carolina. Ten days later, however, on May 19th President Abraham Lincoln countermanded General Hunter's premature order.[12]

Once again Lincoln would remind slave owners that they still could adopt his plan of compensated emancipation. He believed that the "Negro problem" could be solved if all blacks were removed from the country to be colonized elsewhere, and he was in favor of compensating any slave owners who would relinquish their property willingly.[13]

Nevertheless, while still ignoring Lincoln's objections, General Hunter continued with his plan of recruiting blacks into the Union Army. After ordering the conscription of all able-bodied black men aged eighteen to forty-five, he then proceeded to organize the 1st South Carolina Colored Regiment on the Sea Islands of South Carolina.

In August 1862, however, Hunter's short-lived black regiment of Sea Islanders was disbanded due to several insurmountable problems. First, the regiment had no authorization from the War Department; therefore, the men received no pay. Second, the morale of the black soldiers in the Sea Islands was extremely low due to the manner in which the recruits had been impressed into the Army, reminding them of the bitter days when they had been sold and separated from their families. Third, they recalled the dire warnings of their former owners that the Yankees were going to sell them to Cuba. [14]

Even after Secretary of War Edwin Stanton finally authorized the 1st South Carolina Regiment as a Federal unit rather than as a state militia, it was not able to complete its reorganization until 31 January 1863. Consequently, it would become the fifth black regiment in the Union Army, even though it had actually been formed before the 1st Kansas. (15)

As the months passed and as the northern armies penetrated deeper into the South, thousands of runaways sought their "savior," the Union Army. "Reach the Yankees and you will be free," is what they were hearing over the "slave grapevine." Consequently, many "shantytowns" began to sprout around the areas where the Yankee soldiers were garrisoned, such as in North Carolina at Plymouth located inland on the Roanoke River and Roanoke Island located at the mouth of the Albemarle Sound on the eastern coast. (16)

Slaves had been building fortifications for the Confederates on Roanoke Island before Burnside's Expedition took place on 7 February 1862. After the Yankees won the battle, many of the blacks were hired as cooks, woodcutters, teamsters, porters, carpenters, and blacksmiths. (17)

The settlement of blacks that subsequently developed on Roanoke Island was called The Freedmen's Colony under the leadership of Rev. Horace James, a former army chaplain, who was appointed Superintendent of Negro Affairs for the District of North Carolina. (18) Unfortunately, the Utopian colony Rev. James was anticipating in 1863 to serve as a template for future settlements of former slaves was not successful. For one thing, it became much too overcrowded due to the large number of escapees from nearby plantations, especially after a boatload of refugees arrived in April of 1864 during the disastrous Battle of Plymouth.

With the end of the war still nowhere in sight, Frederick Douglass pleaded once again with President Abraham Lincoln to allow blacks to enlist.[19] His prophetic words were: *"Once let the black man get upon his person the brass letters, U.S., let him get an eagle on his button, and a musket on his shoulder and bullets in his pocket, and there is no power on earth which can deny that he has earned the right to citizenship in the United States."* [20]

However, the president still refused. The war would drag on for two long years with mounting casualties and desertions, as well as an unsuccessful draft before Lincoln finally relented.

Following his signing of the Emancipation Proclamation on 1 January 1863, black men on 22 May 1863 were afforded the opportunity to join the ranks of the Union Army, even though the President was harshly criticized by others who doubted that black men could or would fight. However, because he was so desperately in need of their manpower, and in spite of his adamant critics, he established the Bureau of Colored Troops to consist of black regiments led by white officers.[21]

General Orders #143 [22] issued by the Secretary of War, E. D. Townsend, stated:

> *III. Boards will be convened at such posts as may be decided upon by the War Department to examine applicants for commissions to command colored troops, who on application to the Adjutant General, may receive authority to present themselves to the board of examination.*
>
> *IV. No persons shall be allowed to recruit for colored troops except specially authorized by the War Department; and no such authority will be given to persons who have not been examined and passed by a board; nor will such authority be given any one person to raise more than one regiment.*

> *V. The reports of Boards will specify the grade of commission for which each candidate is fit, and authority to recruit will be given in accordance. Commissions will be issued from the Adjutant General's Office when the prescribed number of men is ready for muster into service.*

The first northern regiments of black soldiers were raised in the states of Connecticut and Massachusetts.(23) Enlisting in the latter were the two sons of Frederick Douglass, Charles and Lewis. In addition, hundreds of free black men, even residents of other northern states such as New York and Pennsylvania, hurried to Massachusetts to join the 54th Infantry. From February to May 1863 its ten companies completely filled, creating the first northern colored regiment. Even absconding slaves who had enlisted in the South were sent to the northern regiments, such as North Carolinian Thomas Patience who served in the 5th Massachusetts (Colored) Cavalry.(24)

Who were the white officers who volunteered to train and lead inexperienced black soldiers when there was such a controversy concerning them? Some did so since it would give them an opportunity to raise their rank; for until the Civil War erupted, upward mobility in the United States Army had been frozen. Included was Captain Robert Gould Shaw, who rose to the rank of Colonel by becoming the commander of the 54th Massachusetts (Colored) Infantry.(25) To his credit he also truly believed that black men could and would make good soldiers.

The Colonel's father had questioned his son on the subject of segregation in the army since black soldiers were being relegated to black regiments only. His reply in a letter was that "*any intermingling would have to be preceded by a long process of education. White orderlies made no objection to living in the same tent with black orderlies; but if white volunteers were asked to receive Negroes in their regiments, they would object fiercely.*"[26] Civilians, seemingly, had fewer objections to sharing with blacks than the soldiers had.

Even though segregation was the general rule, a mixed force of Negroes, Indians, and whites won the battle of Elk Creek (Honey Springs) in Oklahoma on 17 July 1863. They were the 1st Kansas Colored Infantry, the 2nd, 6th, and 9th Kansas Cavalry, the 2nd and 3rd Kansas Batteries, and the 2nd and 3rd Kansas Indian Home Guards. [27] After a four-hour engagement, Confederate casualties included 134 killed and wounded while the Federals counted 17 killed and 69 wounded. Because of those figures, the Battle of Elk Creek has been called the "Gettysburg of the West."

Later, an order dated 11 March 1864 and issued by the Adjutant General's office would state that all black regiments thenceforth would be designated by numbers with the word "Colored" included. Except for three from Massachusetts and one from Connecticut, all black regiments were designated "USCT," including the 79th USCT, that originally had been the 1st Kansas Colored Volunteer Infantry, as contrasted to the 5th Massachusetts (Colored) Cavalry, the 54th and 55th Massachusetts (Colored) Infantry, and the 28th Connecticut (Colored) Infantry that kept their state identification. [28]

History books, if indeed they record any information about the United States Colored Troops at all, suggest that the number of those soldiers was anywhere from 100,000 to 300,000. Significant discrepancies exist, however, as is demonstrated by the following sources that offered hypotheses:

The Negro's Civil War: *"By October 20, 1864, there were 140 Negro regiments in the Federal Service with a total strength of 101,950 men.*" [29]

The American Heritage Picture History of the Civil War: *"All told, the Federals put more than 150,000 Negroes into uniform. Many of these regiments were used only for garrison duty, and in many other cases the army saw to it that the colored regiments became little more than permanent fatigue details to relieve white soldiers of hard work, but some units saw actual combat service."* (30)

The Negro in the Civil War: *"A total of 178,895 Negroes served as Federal soldiers in the Civil War."* (31)

Forged in Battle: *"Here were almost 180,000 Afro-Americans, enslaved in the South and discriminated against in the North, who had responded to the call to arms in the hope of creating a better world for themselves, and their children."* (32)

From Slavery to Freedom: *"Enlistment of blacks was, however, a notable success: more than 186,000 had enrolled in the Union Army by the end of the war."* (33)

The Sable Arm: *"Although War Department records show that 178,895 Negro soldiers served, one biography of Ulysses S. Grant states that there were 'about one hundred thousand negroes in the Union Army' while the Dictionary of Army History gives an approximation of 300,000."* **(34)**

A more recent accounting is found, not in a book, but at the center of a granite-paved plaza in Washington, D.C., where not far from the African American Civil War Memorial the bronze "Spirit of Freedom" was unveiled on 18 July 1998.**(35)** Fittingly, it is located at the entrance of the U Street-Cardoza Subway Station at 10th and U Streets in the Shaw section of the nation's capitol. That section of the city has been named in recognition of Colonel Robert Gould Shaw, the brave young commander of the famed Massachusetts 54th (Colored) Infantry who demonstrated its valor in the futile attempt to take from the Confederates Battery Worth in the Charleston, South Carolina, harbor.

That disastrous battle on Morris Beach occurred on 18 July 1863, one hundred and thirty-five years to the day prior to the unveiling of "Spirit of Freedom." Created by Ed Hamilton, (36) a sculptor from Louisville, Kentucky, it honors 209,145 black men and their white officers who served during the Civil War. (37)

In a semi circle it depicts three uniformed black soldiers carrying their rifles and a sailor grasping a ship's wheel. On the opposite side sculpture is a family group with its returning soldier to represent the homes for which the men fought.

"Spirit of Freedom" Monument, Washington, D.C.
Courtesy of Hari Jones

Names of soldiers by regiments are engraved on 155 burnished stainless steel plaques on the *Wall of Honor* that encircles the monument on three sides. The names were obtained from the National Park Service and the National Archives in Washington, D.C.[38] The discrepancy between the figures of the 178,895 reported by the War Department and the 209,145 may be due to more than one man possessing the same name. Also, a soldier may have been transferred from one regiment to another, resulting in being listed twice. [39]

A Civil War Sailors' Database has recently been developed, as well. It contains the names of more than 18,000 sailors who served on nearly 700 integrated naval vessels. This database is the product of a partnership begun in 1993 by the Department of the Navy, the National Park Service, and Howard University in Washington, D.C.

Therefore, with the addition of the Navy list, the presumption might be made that all black soldiers and sailors who served during the Civil War now have been identified. However, there remains a category of black soldiers yet to be enumerated and recognized. **They are those who served in white regiments.** Although the number may not be large, those men were as willing to offer their lives for freedom as were those who served in the segregated regiments. They, too, deserve to be remembered and recognized.

Act of June 27, 1890.

Declaration for Increase of Pension.

☞ Execute this before an officer having a seal.

STATE OF Virginia COUNTY OF Norfolk ss:

On this 22d day of April A. D., 1897, personally appeared before me a Deputy Clerk within and for the County and State aforesaid, Richard West (Claimant's name should be written here.) aged 58 years (Age here.), a resident of Berkley (Place of residence here.) County of Norfolk (Name of County here.) State of Virginia (Name of State here.) who, being duly sworn according to law, declares that he is the identical Richard West (Name of Claimant.) who was enrolled on the 1st day of March (Month.), 1864 (Year.), in Co. I 103rd Regt Pa (Here state rank, Co. and Reg't, if in Military service, or vessel if in the Navy.) in the WAR of the REBELLION and served at least NINETY DAYS, and was HONORABLY DISCHARGED at Newberne NC (Place where discharged.) on the 25th day of June (Month.), 1865 (Year.) and *was not* employed in the Military or Naval service of the United States prior to the 1st day of March (Month.), 1864 (Year.) or subsequent to the ...... day of .... (Month.), 1864 (Year.)

That he is partially (Partially or wholly.) unable to earn a support by manual labor. That he is a pensioner under Certificate No. .... at 6 dollars per month. That his physical condition is such that he believes he is entitled to an increase of pension. That in addition to the disabilities heretofore alleged and claimed for he is disabled by reason of Rheumatism impaired sight and Gun shot wound of left leg which was incurred at Plymouth NC about April 1st (Month.) 1864 (Year.), under the following circumstances: in passing Redout

That said disabilities are not due to vicious habits, and are to the best of his knowledge and belief *permanent*.

That he makes this declaration for the purpose of securing an increase of pension under the provisions of the ACT OF JUNE 27, 1890. He hereby appoints

J. B. CRALLE & CO., Pension Attorneys,
CRALLE BUILDING, 108 C Street, N. W., Washington, D. C.,

his true and lawful attorneys to prosecute his claim, and he hereby agrees to allow said attorneys the lawful fee of Two Dollars when his increase is allowed. That his Postoffice address is Berkley (Claimant's P. O. address here.) County of Norfolk (Name of County here.) State of Virginia (Name of State here.)

Attest two witnesses. { Chas Gibbs; [illegible] }

Richard his X mark West
[Claimant's Signature.]

ATT'Y FILED

Richard West's Pension Record

CHAPTER III

Black Soldiers in White Regiments

In a letter to the editor of the *Civil War News*,[(40)] Civil War historian William Gladstone listed several distinct categories of black men who served in the Union Army:

a. State regiments that maintained their state identification such as the 54th Massachusetts,
b. State regiments who were re-designated in the *Corps d'Afrique*. There were state regiment re-designated from the *Corps d'Afrique* and then into the USCT, plus there were state regiments re-designated into the USCT,
c. U.S. Infantry regiments such as Ullman's Brigade,
d. *Corps d'Afrique* regiments, and of course
e. United States Colored Troops.

To Gladstone's five categories, I respectfully add a sixth. **The black soldiers who served in white regiments.**

A first question asked might be, *"Were the black men who served in white regiments mulattoes whose racial identification could not be determined?"* No doubt many were, being the products of over 140 years of miscegenation. However, others have been racially identified in their military records as "Col'd," "Negro," "African descent (A.D.)," or "contraband," thereby leaving little doubt that, indeed, they were identifiably black men. [(41)]

A second question may be, "*Who, then, were those black soldiers that history has forgotten?*" Mainly they were men who had enlisted in the army in order to fight for the freedom of their race, only to find that they were allocated noncombatant jobs such as cooks and undercooks, thus being segregated within white regiments according to the tasks they were allowed to perform. These soldiers have been forgotten.

The majority of those who joined the army after the Union troops penetrated the South were runaway slaves, the simplest of men living the United States, not even dignified as "men" since for taxation purposes they were counted as 3/5 of a person.[42] They were chattel, someone's property, but because they yearned for freedom, when the opportunity came they fled their bondage in droves.

Contrastingly, northern black men who joined the Union Army were already free men, such as Frederick Douglass' two sons, Lewis and Charles. They are among the thousands whose participation is being remembered on the wall surrounding the "Spirit of Freedom" Memorial.

****

Had the black soldiers who served in the white regiments objected when assigned to such menial jobs as cooking food for the white soldiers in their companies? Certainly they were not experienced with such "women's" work. Usually their enlistment papers would state "laborer" or "farmer" [43] as their former occupation, when not identifying them as "slave." However, objecting was not something blacks were inclined to do, at least not publicly. Perhaps they may have been surprised, though, and possibly even a bit chagrined, since their purpose for joining the army had been to participate in the fight for their freedom.

Had they been disappointed? No doubt. However, with freedom guaranteed if the Union won the war, the majority probably simply followed orders just as they had been doing all of their lives and anxiously waited for the war to end when the promise of freedom would be theirs to claim.

At first, though, all black soldiers were paid less than their white counterparts. Compare the blacks' $10.00 per month with the whites' $13.00. Also, blacks received $3.00 to purchase their clothing, whereas, white soldiers were given $3.50 for theirs. For a year the 54th Massachusetts Infantry in which the Douglass brothers served protested by refusing to accept the insulting pay. Finally, on 1 January 1864 equal pay for all soldiers was granted by the Federal Government.(44) Interestingly, it was the very day of my great grandfather's enlisting at Plymouth, North Carolina.

Stories of interest exist in regards to the enlistment of men African descent, especially prior to General Orders 143 that introduced the segregated regiments and General Orders 323 that dealt specifically with undercooks of African descent. One such man was William Henry Johnson of Norwich, Connecticut, a very dark complexioned free man, who due to his race, had not been allowed to enlist in the local regiment when it responded to the first call for state militia troops to defend Washington for a ninety day-duration; he joined the 2nd Connecticut Volunteer Infantry as an "independent man," an undefined status.

After completing his ninety-day enlistment, he then enlisted in the 8th Connecticut Volunteer Infantry, participating in the first battle between the Union and the Confederacy at Bull Run (Manassas to the Confederates), Virginia, on 21 July 1861 when defeated northern troops were forced to retreat twenty-five miles back to Washington, D.C.

William H. Johnson later took part in the "Burnside Expedition" that captured Roanoke Island, North Carolina, in February of 1862. While with the army he served also as a reporter, sending back nine informative and detailed letters to the editors of a Boston magazine, *The Pine and Palm.* (45)

Other New England black "patriots" were on Roanoke Island, too, as William Henry Johnson's letter alludes to by his signing it as a member of the "8th Colored Volunteers." They were called "patriots" because they were volunteers and not members of the regular army.

Editors of the Pine and Palm, Boston, Mass.—The Burnside expedition has been gloriously successful. The rebels have been defeated and driven from Roanoke Island. On Friday our fleet came to anchor in Albemarle sound at ten o'clock A.M. The rebels fired into the fleet from a battery on the shore. The gunboats responded with vigor.

4 P.M.—The bombardment is progressing with great fury.
5 P.M.--We are gaining upon the rebels; our troops are being landed in small boats in the face of the enemies' batteries.
9 P.M.—We are on the island; the enemy is held in check; hostilities have ceased for the night.
Saturday, 10 A.M.—The battle has been resumed; the rebel land battery is being engaged by our troops; the bombardment is still going on.
1.30 P.M.—The rebels have been driven from the batteries at the point of the bayonet. The field is ours; we are pursuing the rebels.
11 P.M.—Two thousand rebels have unconditionally surrendered. It is the end of one of the bloodiest battles of the campaign.

Our victory has, indeed, been brilliant, but we have paid dearly for it. Our loss is about thirty killed, among whom is a colonel and a lieutenant-colonel, and a number of line officers. We have in the hospital between seventy-five and eighty wounded; they are all doing well. The enemy's loss I have not ascertained, but it has been considerable. I counted ten dead in one battery myself.

O. Jennings Wise, son of General Wise, is one of our prisoners, and he is mortally wounded.

W.H.J.,
Eighth Colored Volunteers

Headquarters, Fort Renno, Roanoke Island, N.C.

In fact, the members of the 8th Colored Volunteers may have been among the same men he wrote about from Annapolis, Maryland, on 11 November 1861:

"The proscribed Americans (and there are many) attached to this regiment have since their encampment here, formed themselves into a defensive association. They propose to cultivate a correct knowledge of the manual of arms and military evolutions, with a view to self-protection. The association is based upon the principles of military discipline, morality and literature; and they hope by a strict observance of the rules and regulations they have adopted to do credit to their people, and honor to themselves.

The name of the association is 'Self-Defenders of Connecticut.' Their officers are: Wm. H. Johnson, Norwich, first officer; Frederick C. Cross, Hartford, second officer; Prince Robinson, Norwalk, third officer. In forming this association, we have been actuated by the conviction that the time is not far distant when the black man of this country will be summoned to show his hand in the struggle for liberty."[46]

Due to illness, William Henry Johnson was forced to leave the army prematurely. Afterwards, he became a recruiter for the first northern colored regiment. He wrote to the following on 15 April 1863 to the editors of the *Standard and Statesman*:

Gentlemen,--I left Albany last Thursday morning with forty-five Negroes for the Fifth [47] *Massachusetts (Colored) Regiment. We arrived at Camp Meigs, Readville, the same evening, and were welcomed by five hundred and odd fully-equipped and well-drilled colored soldiers, under the command of Colonel R. G. Shaw. I handed over my command to the officer of the day, and then proceeded to learn the condition of the camp, the men in the camp and things in general....*"[48]

A barber by trade, he later became a prominent business man in Albany, New York, and was involved in many civic activities. After writing his interesting memoirs in *Autobiography of Dr. William Henry Johnson* published in 1900, he lived another eighteen years.

John Thompson was another black "patriot." He joined the 24th Massachusetts Volunteers. Tragically, though, he was shot accidentally when he had returned home to visit his mother. His funeral was held on 27 December 1861. [49]

Hezekiah Ford Douglass had been a Chicago preacher when he joined Co. G of the 95th Illinois Infantry in July 1862, subsequently fighting in Tennessee and Louisiana. Later he became a recruiter for a black regiment in Louisiana and was promoted to captain of an artillery battery from Kansas, becoming one of the few black men holding commissions in the Union Army. Even so, his army career began when he served in an all-white regiment before the Emancipation Proclamation was signed. [50]

Allen Allensworth had been born a slave in Louisville, Kentucky. After teaching himself to read from the Bible and a Webster Speller, he attempted twice to escape to Canada. He was caught each time and subsequently sold to a slave trader going south. However, he later was able to escape from Mississippi, thereafter traveling north to Illinois. During the Civil War he attached himself to the 44th Illinois Infantry, serving as a corpsman/nurse and went back South with the unit to Tennessee.

He later joined the Union Navy and served aboard several gunboats on the Mississippi River.

His life indeed was remarkable since Allen Allensworth had gone from being a slave to becoming the first black chaplain and the highest ranking black officer in the United States military when he retired as a Lieutenant Colonel in 1906. "Slave, jockey, corpsman/nurse, Civil War gunboat sailor on the Mississippi, businessman, pastor, educator, politician, officer in the United States Army, and chaplain." In 1914, unfortunately, he died in an accident in the newly created black southern California town that was named after him. Today, however, it is the Colonel Allensworth State Historic Park[51] in Tulare County.

****

A mistake, however, is to suggest that Nicholas Biddle, a black man from Pottsville, Pennsylvania, was the first "soldier" to shed blood during the Civil War. He may have been the first man shedding blood, but Nicolas Biddle was not a *bona fide* soldier. Rather, he was a sixty-five year old orderly to Captain James Wren of the Washington Artillerists. When the Artillerists departed for Washington, D.C., to defend the city for a ninety day-duration, Biddle went along with them.

The five companies of First Defenders arrived by train in Baltimore, Maryland, on 18 April 1861. At that time no direct railroad line connected the North to the nation's capitol. Therefore, in order to board a southbound train, the Pennsylvanians were forced to march through Baltimore past crowds of angry pro-secessionists.

Clad in blue, an older black man proudly marched behind the companies. The sight so enraged the spectators that from both sides of the road showers of bricks were hurled. One brick gashed the forehead of Nicolas Biddle, thereby giving him the distinction of being the first man to shed blood in the Civil War.

Ninety years following the Baltimore riot, a bronze plaque was dedicated on the western side of Soldiers' Monument in Garfield Square, Pottsville, Pennsylvania.

It reads: "*In Memory of the First Defenders And Nicholas Biddle, of Pottsville, First Man To Shed Blood In the Civil War. April 18, 1861. Erected by the Citizens of Pottsville, April 18, 1951.*" **(52)**

Nicholas Biddle's story needs to be documented so his participation in the Civil War is not misconstrued. He was not the first "soldier" to shed his blood. Also, his story needs to be recorded so future generations will know that Nicholas Biddle was a black man. No one would know that fact by reading the race-less inscription on the plaque in Pottsville, Pennsylvania.

****

When the Union Army began penetrating the South, hordes of slaves absconded from where they were being held in bondage. The runaway slaves, at first called "refugees," but later "contrabands," were utilized in support roles by the Union Army, thereby freeing the white soldiers from having to perform menial tasks.

As we have noted, President Lincoln signed the Emancipation Proclamation on 1 January 1863 that finally gave black men the right to join the Union Army and many rushed to answer the call. From as far away as California they enlisted. One such recruit was George Rohanan who was mustered into the 2nd California Cavalry on 13 February 1865 at Sacramento. **(53)**

However, the jobs of cook and undercook were the ones most often relegated to the black soldiers who joined white regiments, regardless of whether the men had been contraband or free. Every company had to have cooks and the eager-to-serve blacks were given the job.

General Orders 323 clearly stated that the enlisted cooks were "soldiers." [54] Were those black soldiers allowed any other jobs? Some were, such as Allen Allenworth who at one time had been a corpsman/nurse in the 44th Illinois Infantry. Records of four of the sixteen black cooks in the 1st Alabama Cavalry indicate they had served as teamsters.

Perhaps Charles Graffell may have served as a blacksmith in the 2nd California Cavalry since that was his trade. He was a free man born in Cincinnati, Ohio, whose family had moved to California when he was six years old. As a very young boy, he enlisted in the Union Army in Sacramento on 3 January 1865.

He was discharged at Drum Barracks, California, on 26 December 1865 per S.O. No. 39, Department of Pacific. According to his business card, following the war he became a "veterinary dentist" in Red Bluffs, California. Charles L. Graffell died in 1930.

****

C. GRAFFELL [55]

OCTOGENARIAN'S OBITUARY

Last Call is Answered by War Veteran

Charles Graffell, 80, who answered President Lincoln's call for boy volunteers when but 14 years old, responded to his last call shortly after 10:00 o'clock last night. The Civil War veteran became ill at 1:30 o'clock yesterday afternoon and passed away at his home on Jackson Street nine hours later.

Although born in Ohio, Graffell moved to California when but six years of age. For the past 74 years he has resided in California of which 53 were spent in Red Bluff where he was a blacksmith and horse-shoer.

In addition to his wife, Mrs. Harriet Graffell, the deceased is survived by six children. They are: Mrs. Edna (S/R Edwina) Allen of Reno, Nevada; Newton and Jesse Graffell of Seattle Washington; Mrs. Sarah Fields of Portland, Oregon; Mrs. Annielane MacArthur of Los Angeles; and Mrs. Crystal Graffell of San Francisco. A sister, Mrs. Sally Oliver of Oakland, California and nine grandchildren also survive.

****

OCTOGENERIAN

MILITARY FUNERAL FOR CHARLES GRAFFELL

With the Rev. C. M. Julian, minister of the Red Bluff Methodist Church officiating, impressive military funeral services were held yesterday for Charles Graffell, 80, Civil War veteran, for 74 years a resident of California, who died at his home late Friday night.

Burial was at Oak Hill Cemetery where a firing squad in command of Col. E. A. Lewis and composed of Sam Reed, Max Holiday, Charles W. Pramme, W. H. Ludwig, and Henry J. Schafer, members of the Spanish War veterans, fired a salute over the grave. Taps were sounded by Douglas Thorpe.

At the service in the chapel, music was provided by Mrs. Netherland and Mr. and Mrs. Francis Mitchell. The pallbearers were: G.H. Martin, Henry Love, Charles Coffey, and Joseph Clinton of Red Bluff and H. P. Davis and Ben Harris of Chico.

CHAPTER IV

Discovery

The names of the black soldiers who served in white regiments have not been hidden deliberately for the past 143 years. In fact, the names of colored cooks are easily found at the end of individual state regimental rosters, and access to their military records and pensions can be obtained from the National Archives in Washington, D.C. Most historians, however, were not even aware that black men had served in white regiments. Therefore, not many persons had been looking for them prior to July 1998, except, perhaps, their descendants like my father's brother, Robert Patience, who visited the National Archives in 1932. When I was viewing my great grandfather's military records, I was surprised and pleased to discover Uncle Bob's signature as a researcher two years after his grandfather's death.

How has the information concerning the presence of the black soldiers in white regiments become known to the public? The answer to that question lay in an article published in the *Washington Post* during the spring of 1998. It contained information about a new monument scheduled to be unveiled in July to honor the black soldiers who had served during the Civil War.

Since my great grandfather had served in that war, I became very excited when I read about the eleven-foot bronze monument that would be surrounded by a granite wall of individual stainless steel plaques engraved with the names, regiments, and companies of the black soldiers and their white officers. I was so looking forward to seeing my great grandfather's name, **Crowder Patience,** engraved on the wall.

The Washington Post also reported that the names of the soldiers could be retrieved from the National Parks Database.

However, when I typed the name of my ancestor, the surprising response was, "*No known soldier.*"

Why, how could that be? I know exactly where he is buried in the cemetery in West Pittston, Pennsylvania. How many times during my lifetime had I seen the GAR stanchion [56] next to my great grandfather's Union tombstone where it has stood since 1930? Therefore, to read on my computer screen the words, "*No known soldier,*" was, indeed, quite mystifying to me.

There was no doubt whatsoever in my mind that my great grandfather had been a Civil War veteran because when I was a child, every Decoration (Memorial Day) I would accompany his daughters, my deceased grandfather's sisters, when they would decorate their father's grave with fresh flowers. The spot in the West Pittston Cemetery is easily located for it is identified by a GAR stanchion and an American flag. Annually for each Memorial Day commemoration, the local American Legion chapter replaces the old and tattered flags on the graves of veterans.

One of my grandfather's sisters, Lillian Patience Cuff, moved into my home in New Jersey when she was ninety-one years old, and lived until almost her 103rd birthday in 1986. Needless to say, I asked her many questions about her parents, some she could answer, but many she could not. She would say, "*Juanita, back in those days we didn't ask our parents a lot of questions.*" However, what knowledge I have about my Civil War ancestor, I received mainly from Aunt Lillie.

During her lifetime, she had in her possession a small black tin box in which she would store small items important to her, such as yellowed newspaper clippings of family obituaries. While she was living, I had not known of the existence of the box and was surprised to find it among her belongings following her death. Safely stored away in that "treasure box" were copies of her father's discharge record that had been used when he applied for a Civil War veteran's pension. She had probably forgotten she possessed the document because she had never discussed it with me, curious as I was.

So after reading that surprising message on my computer screen in 1998, I checked Aunt Lillie's treasure box to ascertain the name of her father's regiment. It had not been stored in my memory, even though I had seen it many times when I lived in West Pittston. **The 103rd Pennsylvania Volunteers**. Then when I accessed my computer for the roster of that regiment, I readily found my great grandfather's name listed there. His name is not listed in the National Parks Database because he had not served in one of the segregated 166 USCT regiments, or the *Corps d' Afrique* of Louisiana, or the three black Massachusetts regiments, or the one Connecticut that retained their state designation.

Of course, had I been able to check his tombstone in the West Pittston Cemetery, I easily could have retrieved that pertinent military information. However, when I began this research, I was not in my hometown. Rather, I was in Alexandria, Virginia.

.

I quickly came to the conclusion that I needed to attend the symposium I read about in the *Washington Post*. It was held on 15 July 1998, three days prior to the unveiling of the monument at the Shaw Metro Station at U Street in Washington, D.C. Descendants of black Civil War veterans were invited to attend the events over several days, and hundreds would travel from many parts of the country. Serving on the panel for the Wednesday symposium were a number of very knowledgeable archivists, authors, historians, politicians, professors, and others who discussed their particular areas of expertise concerning the thousands of black soldiers who had served during the Civil War.

As I was attentively listening to each speaker, I began to realize that the only black soldiers being honored by the monument were members of the USCT, the *Corps d' Afrique*, the three black regiments from Massachusetts, and the single one from Connecticut. Such criteria did not include my Civil War ancestor who had served in "none of the above."

Therefore, when the Q&A portion of the symposium was opened, I stepped to the microphone to pose this question to the panelists, *"Have you retrieved from the National Archives the names of the black soldiers who served in white regiments?"*

After several moments passed, the answer I received was, *"No, because there weren't any."* Again, here was another very surprising response to one of my questions, since I knew of at least one who had served in a white regiment. Crowder Pacien, my identifiably "Col'd" ancestor, had been in the 103rd Pennsylvania Volunteer regiment, and that morning I had placed in my briefcase the necessary documentation as proof.

After showing my great grandfather's discharge record to the panelists and after seeing the looks of surprise and hearing the doubt from a number of them, I realized that my family knew of a little known historical fact that needed to be shared with others. **That black soldiers had served also in white regiments during the Civil War**.

So, as I was taking my seat again, I began forming a hypothesis. *"If there had been one black soldier in one white regiment, then perhaps there were more."*

This book is the proof that there were.

CHAPTER V

Research

So, following the symposium on 15 July 1998, my research for this book commenced, beginning with my ancestor, Crowder Patience, an eighteen year-old runaway slave, who had enlisted in the Union Army on 1 January 1864 at Plymouth, North Carolina. It has taken ten years for me to gather the names of the hundreds of forgotten black soldiers who are presented here.

Some died while serving, while others were captured and remanded back to slavery until the end of the war. The Confederacy had been infuriated by the Union's making soldiers out their "property:" rebellious runaway slaves. President Jefferson Davis had ordered in 1862 that all Negro slaves captured while bearing arms were to be returned to their owners. Union officials, however, insisted that the captured blacks be treated as prisoners of war.

Many black soldiers like my ancestor survived and became veterans. Crowder Patience was one of the fortunate to obtain a pension from the United States Government, since many veterans, both white and black, were denied.

I was never in the presence of my great grandfather because he passed away two years before I was born. However, I did know his wife who died when I was eight years old. Most of the information about him, however, came from their daughter Lillian. So what I know about my Civil War ancestor came from prodding her for information and also from a newspaper article published by the *Pittston Gazette* in 1928 when Crowder Patience had been interviewed two years prior to his death. [57]

Another surprise materialized when I was perusing my great grandfather's discharge record that had been stored safely in Aunt Lillie's "treasure box." I discovered that his surname was spelled differently (Pacien)[58] than it is on his tombstone (Patience), the spelling used by his descendants, making me wonder who in his immediate family, other than Aunt Lillie, might have been aware of that fact. She may not have been as surprised as I, though, since his name was spelled several different ways on the various pension records (Pacient, Patient) she may have read. However, I have no idea if she or her siblings ever had an interest in their father's military records.

What the Pennsylvania Patience family knew about their North Carolina slave/soldier ancestor was minimal since many former slaves did not discuss their pasts with their children. Crowder Pacien/Patience was one such man. North Carolina had been his "other" life and he chose not to revisit it. In his "new" life, he was a proud citizen of the small northeastern Pennsylvania borough where in 1883 he chose to rear his family.

Whether Crowder had discussed with his new family anything about the old one he had left behind, I will never know. However, when I discovered on the wall of the monument the name of Thomas Patience who served in the 5th Massachusetts Cavalry, I wondered if he might be Crowder's brother, especially since I discovered that both had been born in Chowan Country, North Carolina, and both possessed the same unusual surname (spelled "Pashons" on some of Thomas' military and pension records). Since both men had been illiterate slaves, during their enlistments their surname had been written phonetically as it sounded to the recruiting agent.

Thomas Patience returned to Chowan County following the war, but Crowder did not. Because Thomas had applied for a pension, I was able to learn that he had been born on the Briol's farm near Edenton, North Carolina.[59] Crowder had told his children that he had been born in Edenton, North Carolina. The two veterans may well have been brothers. Even the description of the two old men recorded on their pension applications is similar, especially the full head of white hair, definitely a Patience family trait. If I could locate one of Thomas' male descendants, a DNA test possibly could prove or disprove a family relationship.

****

Crowder had shared with his family the locale where he had been born, and also the fact that at the age of eighteen he had run away to join the Union Army. His children and grandchildren (one being my father) knew of their ancestor's participation in the G.A.R. because for many years they had watched from the sidelines as he marched proudly with his comrades in the annual Memorial Day parade.(60) Today his descendants, even to the seventh generation, can read the words still clearly engraved on his tombstone: *Crowder Patience 103rd Pennsylvania Infantry, Co. C* as proof of his service,

For even further proof, the roster of the 103rd Pennsylvania Volunteers records:

> *"Pacien, Crowder, Private, Company C., Mustered age 18, April 4-1864-June 24, 1865. Cook, colored, apparently escaped capture following Battle of Plymouth, North Carolina, April 20, 1864."* (61)

****

The 103rd had originated in 1861 at Camp Orr on the Armstrong County Campgrounds in Kittatinny, Pennsylvania, near Pittsburgh. During the Civil War, white regiments mainly were composed of local men, oftentimes family members and neighbors. The 101st Pennsylvania, for instance, was called the "Brothers' Regiment" because of the number of sets of brothers it contained. (62)

During 1863-64 both the 101st and 102nd Pennsylvania Volunteers were garrisoned at Plymouth, North Carolina, where the runaway slave Crowder Pacien enlisted on 1 January 1864 for a three year-duration. He was mustered into Co. C of the 103rd Pennsylvania according to General Orders 73. Following the end of the war, he was mustered out of his company at New Bern, North Carolina on 25 June 1865. Soon after, on 13 July 1865 at Harrisburg, Pennsylvania, with thirty-five of the initial 128 members of Co. C., he received his final discharge. **(63)** I cannot possibly imagine the degree of excitement that may have been experienced by that nineteen year-old former slave as he traveled from what he had known in North Carolina to what was awaiting him as a free man in Pennsylvania.

****

For sixty-five years Crowder Pacien/Patient/Patience would be an active member of the GAR in Wyoming Valley, Pennsylvania. As long as he was able, he would participate in the annual Memorial Day Parade as a 1928 article from the *Pittston Gazette* reported.

"Few days of the year carry more meaning with them than Memorial Day. Once in each twelve months it is observed and throughout the land the disappearing ranks of the Blue and Gray form in line for the parade of honor to their departed comrades. Sixty-three years have passed and few of the heroes remain.

As the lines are formed this year and the veterans group in the cars which will carry them along the line of march, to no one present will such a stream of memories return as to one wearer of the Blue from Exeter. To no other man in Wyoming Valley has such a great wealth and variety of experiences been vouchsafed.

An old and respected colored man is the one in mind. Now eighty-two years of age, a slave in the South before the war, a soldier in the Union Army, and a farmer of Wyoming Valley. Crowder Pacient is the name of this respected resident.

He has kept up his active membership in the G.A.R., attends the meetings whenever able to do so, meets his old comrades of the war regularly and hopes to be able to take part in Memorial Day parade this year. He wasn't sure he could, but he was going to try hard. His place would be hard to fill and he will be sorely missed if not there.

The natural romance and interest which surrounds this old man from the South produce many legends concerning him through the section in which he lives. The most popular is that Jesse Carpenter (64) *found him on the battlefield. It claims he ran up to Carpenter in the midst of battle, seeking assistance and remained with him to be brought home.*

Crowder Pacient went into the Union Army of his own accord and was honorably discharged.

He received a monthly pension from the United States Government. His reason for applying was "rheumatism," a common complaint for many older veterans who applied for and received "invalid" pensions. He died on 30 January 1930 of apoplexy as a result of a "cold and gripp" and was buried on 3 February 1930 in the West Pittston Cemetery.

Crowder Patience was 83 years, one month, and five days old. **(65)**

****

On 12 February 2001 the National Civil War Museum at Harrisburg, Pennsylvania, was dedicated in Grand Opening ceremonies. A "Walk of Valor" had been designed, created of bricks individually engraved with the name of a Civil War soldier. Each state section within the "Walk" is identified with a granite plaque on which is the number of men who served from it, as well as the number of men who died. Many descendants have taken the opportunity to honor their Civil War ancestors by purchasing a brick in their honor.

One brick has been engraved with: ***"Crowder Pacien, Co. C 103rd Reg PA Vol Inf US."*** Due to that visible record, there can be no doubt that a man identified by his military records to be "Col'd," had been a member of a white Union regiment during the Civil War. [66]

****

After researching the Battle of Plymouth that took place 17-20 April 1864 and learning that the Union troops had been defeated, one might wonder how an eighteen year-old runaway slave could have escaped capture when all of the white soldiers (dubbed "Plymouth Pilgrims") [67] had either been killed or captured to be transported by train to Andersonville Prison in Georgia. The explanation of my ancestor's serendipitous escape was discovered by researching journals, letters, and books penned by white soldiers whose regiments had been garrisoned at Plymouth, North Carolina.

Luther Dickey, a corporal from the 103rd Pennsylvania Infantry, recorded that on 2 January 1864, the day after Crowder Pacien enlisted, Company C to which he was assigned sailed east across the Albemarle Sound to Roanoke Island.[68] The policy was that one company of each of the nine regiments garrisoned at Plymouth would always be on Roanoke Island, to block entrance to and from the Atlantic Ocean, thereby preventing the Confederates from exporting their cotton and tobacco while importing arms with Europe, as well as cutting off their supply of the necessary salt for manufacturing gunpowder.

The remaining nine companies of the 103rd were garrisoned inland at the small port of Plymouth on the south bank of the Roanoke River. Fortunately for Private Crowder Pacien, when the battle at Plymouth had erupted on 17 April 1864, he was with Co. C safely garrisoned on Roanoke Island. This pertinent information is not found on the roster of the 103rd Volunteers where no explanation is given for: *"apparently escaped capture following the Battle of Plymouth."*

Seige of Plymouth Historic Marker
Plymouth, North Carolina
From the author's collection

At the time of the disastrous siege at Plymouth, in four of the nine garrisoned regiments there, eleven "Col'd" cooks, were present, all ranked as privates. [(69)] Four who served in the 103rd Pennsylvania Infantry Regiment Veterans Volunteers were:

Dolphus Garrett, Co. K, was born in Bertie County, North Carolina. He was age eighteen, 5'5" in height, and listed as a laborer. Instead of "slave," many records used "laborer" or "farmer." He had enlisted for three years at Plymouth, but unfortunately, he was captured at the Battle of Plymouth, recorded as missing in action, and was perhaps killed while trying to escape. [(70)]

Samuel Granville, Co. B, was mustered in on 13 November 1863. Born in Martin County, North Carolina, he was age twenty-five, 5'5" in height, and by occupation had been a laborer. He, too, was recorded as missing in action at the Battle of Plymouth, supposedly killed. [(71)]

Titus Hardy (*a.k.a.* Titus McRae), Co. K, was mustered in on 1 December 1863 and again on 1 March 1864. Born in Tyrell County, North Carolina, he was age thirty-one, 5'4" in height, and listed as a laborer. Reported missing in action following the Battle of Plymouth, he had been taken prisoner and, subsequently, reclaimed by his master. After escaping again he re-enlisted under an alias. The military records for Titus Hardy/McRae include his having received a pension following the war. [(72)]

Richard West, Co. I, was mustered in on 3 March 1864. He had been a slave born in Bertie County, North Carolina, and was 5'7" at age twenty-one. Captured during the Battle of Plymouth, he was sent to Rainbow Banks near Hamilton, North Carolina, to work on fortifications at Fort Branch. Escaping at his first opportunity, he reported to Co. C of the 103rd Pennsylvania being reconstituted on Roanoke Island. On 25 June 1865, he was discharged at New Bern, North Carolina. His military records include a monthly invalid pension issued in 1892, which continued until his death on 2 November 1910, in Norfolk, Virginia. (73)

Because of the continuing controversy over whether black soldiers had been "massacred" on 20 April 1864 by the Confederates following the Battle of Plymouth, the name of Richard West resurfaced when an article by Weymouth Jordan and Gerald Thomas was published in 1998. (74) West's complete records are filed at the Port O' Plymouth Museum in Plymouth, North Carolina. His race is not mentioned in Broadfoot's Pennsylvania volume, but he has been identified among the others as a black cook at Plymouth during the battle.

Black soldiers from other regiments present at the battle include:

Alec Johnson of the 85th N. Y. Infantry, who was killed when he refused to surrender, according to a post war account; (75)

Henry Pugh of the 85th N. Y. Infantry, who at first was reported missing, but later rejoined his unit; (76)

Nelson Sheppard of the 24th N. Y. Battery, who was taken prisoner and severely whipped because he had been a guide for the Yankees. He was sent in ball and chains to Weldon to work on the fortifications there. Finally, in the fall of 1864, he was able to make his escape to join his company which was being reconstituted at Roanoke Island; (77)

George Washington of 24th N. Y. Battery who escaped capture following the Battle of Plymouth and also rejoined his unit; [(78)]

John Rolack/Rolac (Roulhac) of the 85th N.Y. Infantry, [(79)] a hazel-eyed, light haired mulatto who died at Andersonville Prison and was buried in grave #9549. [(80)]

When the Confederates reported Rolack's death, they did not identify him as "Col'd," but his Union records already had racially identified him. He is the only known fugitive slave buried at Andersonville Prison and then only because he was mistaken for white since the Rebels would not have included him with the other captives from Plymouth. Rather, they would have sent him back to his owner according to President Jefferson Davis' orders.

By intent, newspapers reported nothing concerning the fate of blacks at Plymouth. Fearful of the Federal reaction to captured black soldiers and sailors being returned to their masters rather than being treated as prisoners of war, President Davis had directed North Carolina's Governor Zebulon Vance to make certain that such information would never reach the newspapers.

General Braxton Bragg sent the following dispatch to Governor Vance:

"The president directs that the negroes captured by our forces be turned over to you for the present, and he requests of you that if, upon investigation, you ascertain that any of them belong to citizens of North Carolina, you will cause them to be restored to their respective owners. If any are owned in other states, you will please communicate to me their number and the names and places of residence of their owners, and have them retained in strict custody until the President's views in reference to such may be conveyed to you.

To avoid as far as possible all complications with the military authorities of the United States in regard to the disposition which will be made of this class of prisoners, the President respectfully requests Your Excellency to take the necessary steps to have the matter of such disposition kept out of the newspapers of the State, and in every available way to shun its obtaining any publicity as far as consistent with the proposed restoration. (81)

R | 85 | N. Y.

John Rolack

, Co. C, 85 Reg't N. Y. Infantry.

Appears on **Regimental Return**

for November, 1863.

Present or absent

Gain or loss Gain - Enlisted in the Regiment

Date Nov. 12, 1863.

Place Plymouth, N. C.

Remarks: Under cook - African descent.

Proof of John Rolack's racial identification

MEMORANDUM FROM PRISONER OF WAR RECORDS. No.

(This blank to be used only in the arrangement of said records.)

NAME.	RANK.	No. of Reg't.	State.	Arm of Service.	Co.	Records of—	Vol.	Page.	Vol.	Page.
				—	C		42½	20		
Rolack, J	P	85	N.Y		L	M. R	17	125	3	223

Captured at , 186 , confined at Richmond, Va., , 186 .

" " And. Ga date not given

Admitted to Hospital at Andersonville, Ga Sep 20" 64 Dysentery

where he died Sep 23' , 1864, of Scorbutus No of grave 9549

Paroled at , 186 ; reported at Camp Parole, Md., , 186 .

No. 12715

Copied by TMcF

John Rolack's Death Record from Andersonville

The names of those black soldiers who had enlisted at Plymouth, North Carolina, were the first of the hundreds I have since discovered after being told there had been none in white regiments. Because my ancestor had served in a Pennsylvania regiment, I chose that state to commence my search for additional names.

The Military Barracks [(82)] in Carlisle, Pennsylvania, seemed the likeliest place to visit. Needing information on how to proceed in that vast repository of military records, I approached a knowledgeable looking gentleman, a Dr. Charles Summers. I told him that I was looking for information concerning black soldiers who had served in white regiments during the Civil War. I also shared with him that I had been told by several historians there had been none, even though I personally knew of at least one.

Dr. Summers replied that he did have some information for me and went off to retrieve a folder containing the military records of Charles Graffell who served in the 2nd California Cavalry. Interestingly, in 1948 a descendant of Graffell had requested his ancestor's military information, and what was most amazing to me, is that Dr. Summers remembered that request fifty-one years later.

I asked him how he could remember that particular file from so long ago. He said it was because at that time he had been surprised to learn there had been any black soldiers integrated into white regiments in the Civil War. Unfortunately, he was unable to provide me with any other names.

However, believing there may have been others, Dr. Summers directed me to Samuel Bates' *History of the Pennsylvania Volunteers* [83] where I was able to find exactly the information I was seeking. I discovered names of other black soldiers who also had served in white Pennsylvania regiments.

The following "Col'd" soldiers are recorded in the Index which is the key to the records of the individual Union volunteer soldiers abstracted after the war from the official documents created during the war. These names have been cross referenced with Bates. However, there are additional black privates named in the Pennsylvania Index, but not found in Bates.

Atus, James	57th	Infantry	
Bullard, Aaron	47th	Infantry	Co. D
Bullard, John	47th	Infantry	Co. D
Clark, William	7th	Cavalry	Co. G
Clemens, Samuel	7th	Cavalry	Co. H
Cloud, Solomon	28th	Infantry	Co. B
Cobb, William	28th	Infantry	Co. B
Cooper, William	7th	Cavalry	Co. I
Day, Alfred	3rd	Cavalry	Co. G
Elick, John	7th	Cavalry	Co. D
Flander, Samuel	55th	Infantry	Co. K
Folk, Thomas	11th	Cavalry	Co. M
Fisher, William	15th	Cavalry	Co. H
Freeman, George	103rd	Infantry	Co. I
Graham, David	7th	Cavalry	Co. M
Hickman, James	7th	Cavalry	Co. C
Holmes, Daniel	7th	Cavalry	Co. I
Johnson, Henry	101st	Infantry	Co. C
Jones, James	19th	Cavalry	
Langley, George	11th	Cavalry	Co. A
Lee, Edward	7th	Cavalry	Co. L
MacDryfuss, Shelby	7th	Cavalry	Co. F
Mayfield, John	11th	Cavalry	Co. A
McDonald, Alfred	7th	Cavalry	Co. M
Mercer, Raymond	58th	Infantry	Co. A
Moore, Hamilton	7th	Cavalry	Co. K

Myott (Wyott), John	101st	Infantry	Co. I
Oakley, Peter	15th	Cavalry	Co. I
Patton, David	7th	Cavalry	Co E
Pete, Thomas	28th	Infantry	Co. B
Pigg, Benjamin	15th	Cavalry	Co. E
Rice, David	7th	Cavalry	Co. A
Robinson, Cornelius	1st Res. Lt. Art'y		Batt'y E
Robison, Philip	55th	Infantry	Co. H
Robison, Toby	55th	Infantry	Co. H
Rooker, Handy	15th	Cavalry	Co. C
Sanders, Ben	55th	Infantry	Co. K
Small, Napoleon	55th	Infantry	Co. C
Smith, Jonas	58th	Infantry	Co. D
Smith, Joseph	55th	Infantry	Co. B
Smith, Philip	7th	Cavalry	Co. F
Snipe, Abraham	55th	Infantry	
Snipe, Ishmael	55th	Infantry	Co. B
Stewart, Stephen	7th	Cavalry	Co. K
Suggs, Henry	58th	Infantry	Co. B
Thomas, John	19th	Cavalry	Co. A
Townson, Randel	7th	Cavalry	Co. E.
Wilson, Thomas	3rd	Cavalry	Co. G.

Continuing my research to other states, I discovered the names of many "Col'd" cooks and undercooks listed in the index to the Compiled Military Service Records (CMSR) located at the National Archives in Washington, D.C. Since the early 1960s the index has been available in approximately 1300 reels of microfilm arranged first by state and then alphabetically by name. Since the thirty volumes of *Roster of the Union Soldiers 1861-1865* by Broadfoot Publishers contain much of that information, they were my next source.

However, to be able to discover the name of every black man who had served in a white regiment during the Civil War is a daunting, if not impossible, task. One problem confronting a researcher is that at the National Archives the racial identification of some cooks is not recorded on the envelopes that contain their military information. Such is true of Henry

Johnson and John Wyott (Myott) of the 101st Pennsylvania Infantry, as well as Titus Hardy/McRae and Richard West of the 103rd Pennsylvania Infantry.[(84)] Therefore, if looking only at the front of the envelopes, a researcher would not know that those particular men were "Col'd."

Another problem is that a number of mulattos were light-complexioned enough to pass as white men, as was John Rolack/Rolac (Roulhac). Therefore, unless descendants of those particular men reveal the fact that their ancestors had served in the Civil War, their racial identity cannot be proven. Aquilla Lett, for instance, of the 13th Michigan Infantry has no racial identification listed on his military records, but one of his great grand daughters, genealogist Peggy Sawyer Williams [(85)] of Detroit, Michigan, submitted his name, as well as other three mulattos[(86)]:

William Dudley Fox who at age thirty-three was drafted on 14 November 1863 into the 2nd Michigan Cavalry, Company F and after participating in several battles was mustered out in Macon, Georgia on 17, August 1865;

Benjamin F. Guy who at age eighteen was a member of the 16th Michigan Infantry, Company F. A GAR marker is on his grave, but the date of his death is not known;

Aquilla Lett who enlisted at age thirty-five in the 13th Michigan Infantry, Company K that marched from Chattanoga, Tennessee and Savannah, Georgia, ending in Washington, D.C. where he was mustered out on 8 June, 1865. He died on 20 February 1902;

Hopkins West [(87)] who at age twenty-seven joined the 13th Michigan Infantry, Company K. As a knowledgeable comrade, he signed an affidavit to verify Aquilla Lett's claims for a disability pension. His burial place is unknown.

Sept 24/87

The first I noticed of Mr Aquilla Lett
Complaining was while laying in the
swamps at Savannah Georgia.
he was excused from duty or work
on the fort. he having the piles and
Rheumatism. piles Caused by hard marching
and the Rheumatism caused by laying
exposed to the weather in the swamps
And he was complaining at different
times on the march from Savannah
to Raleigh and to washington

Very Respectfully
Hopkins West.

Hopkins West's letter in support of Aquilla Lett's claim

Four additional mulatto soldiers were the Still brothers of Meigs County, Ohio, the great-grand uncles of the late Fred W. Crenshaw, Sr. A retired Air Force Sergeant Major from Suitland, Maryland, he was a member of the Brooks-Grant Camp Number 7, Sons of Union Veterans of the Civil War, Meigs County, Ohio. Before his untimely death in 1999, he, too, had been vitally interested in obtaining recognition for the forgotten black men who had served in white regiments during the Civil War.

Fred Crenshaw's great-uncles were: [(88)]

David Still of the 63rd Ohio Infantry Co. C who served from 25 October 1861 until his death on 5 May 1862;

Andrew Jackson Still, Co. C of the 9th West Virginia Infantry, who served from November 1861 until January 1865;

George Washington Still, Co. I of the 13th West Virginia Infantry, who served from October 1863 to June 1865;

Henry C. Still of the 9th West Virginia Infantry Co. E who served from December 1861 to June 1865. He had re-enlisted in January 1864 as a veteran. Then on 9 May 1864, he was wounded and captured at the Battle of Cloyds Mountain, Virginia. His pension file indicated that he received injuries while a prisoner at Andersonville Prison.

These men returned to their families and back into their "colored" communities following the Civil War. However, many others did not.

Four of Sally Hemings' grandsons, the sons of Madison and Eston, served in the Union Army. Madison's family in Chillicothe, Ohio, remained in the black community. Eston's sons did not.

Madison's son, William Beverly Hemings served in the 73rd Ohio Volunteer Infantry from Chillicothe, Ohio. (89) Another son, Thomas Eston Hemings unfortunately died of battle wounds at Andersonville Prison. (90)

John Wayles Jefferson, the eldest son of Eston Hemings who after leaving Charlottesville, Virginia, changed his surname to Jefferson, entered the Union Army on 26 August 1861 in Madison, Wisconsin. As a white man, he quickly rose in rank, eventually taking command of the 8th Wisconsin Infantry. In 1863 he was promoted to Lieutenant Colonel and in 1864 to Colonel. (91) His younger brother, Beverly Jefferson, served briefly in the 1st Wisconsin Infantry, Company E for three months. (92)

In 1902 the *Scioto Gazette* published an article about Eston Hemings Jefferson. "A Sprig of Jefferson was Eston Hemings." The subheading was: "The Gazette's Delver Into the Past Brings Up a Romantic Story….Was Natural Son of the Sage of Monticello; Had the Traits of Good Training."

A reporter wrote, "*and I saw and talked with one of the sons, during the Civil War, who was then wearing the silver leaves of a lieutenant colonel, and in command of a fine regiment of white men from a north-western state. He begged me not to tell the fact that he had colored blood in his veins, which he said was not suspected by any of his command; and of course I did not.*" (93)

Due to the controversy over the paternity of Sally Hemings' children, that particular family's genealogy has been studied, especially in recent years due to the use of DNA testing. (94) Today many thousands of other Americans have similar racial backgrounds without even knowing it because their mulatto ancestors passed successfully into the white world.

****

Since the majority of black soldiers who served in white regiments had been cooks and undercooks, an interested researcher can visit the National Archives in Washington, D.C., to study the military records of cooks not identified by their race in Broadfoot's *Roster of Union Soldiers*. To do so, however, is a very time consuming task.

First of all, for each soldier one wishes to research, an inquiry form has to be filled out and turned in at a desk on the first floor. On most days at 10:00 a.m., 11:00 a.m., 12 noon, and 2:00 p.m. the requested information will be pulled from the files, but only a mere four documents at a time. Thursday is the exception when the library is opened later hours. Files are not pulled on Saturdays.

In order to study the requested information, the researcher must go to the second floor Research Room. There, one's special Archives Research identification has to be shown in order to gain entrance. Such permission must be obtained beforehand on the first floor where one has his/her photograph taken for an identification card. All belongings must be stowed in a locker room down the hall because all you can take into the research room is yourself and some money for the copy machines. Not even an outside jacket is allowed although the room can be quite chilly at times in order to preserve the valuable records. Pencils and paper are provided for note taking. No pens allowed.

****

The purpose of my research at the National Archives was to determine the race of each cook not racially identified in Broadfoot's *Roster of Union Soldiers* which I used first to find soldiers listed as regimental cooks and undercooks according to General Order 323. Before taking the last step of checking the names listed at the Archives, at home I would check Ancestry.com and the Civil War Database first to see if racial identification is noted on either. In some cases it is.

When it was not, my thoroughness required me to investigate the military records of cooks and undercooks. This information is filed in individual envelopes where I searched for any clue to determine whether or not the subject is or is not one of the black soldiers who served in a white regiment. On hundreds of envelopes, I looked for such identifying words such as: Col'd, contraband, Negro, or African descent/A.D. If I did not find any such words, then I looked for the physical description of the soldier: "black eyes, black hair, black complexion." [(95)]Therefore, for each soldier I investigated by his envelope, I was able to conclude that he was one of the forgotten soldiers who had served in white regiments.

In today's world, of course, such descriptions are not limited to identifying African Americans only. However, most men serving in the Union Army were identified as either "white" or "Col'd," such as Samuel Jones, an undercook who served in the 8th Connecticut Infantry. No mention is made of his race in Broadfoot, but his physical description on his military records leaves no doubt. "*Black eyes, black hair, black complexion.*"

J | 8 | Conn

Samuel Jones

Appears with rank of Undercook on

Muster In and Descriptive Roll of a Detachment of U. S. Vols. forwarded

for the 8 Reg't Ct Inf. Roll dated

Manchester, Va, May 6, 1865.

Where born Amelia, Va.

Age 21 years; occupation Laborer

When enlisted May 1, 1865.

Where enlisted Manchester, Va

For what period enlisted 3 years.

Eyes Blk; hair Blk

Complexion Blk; height 5 ft. 3 in.

When mustered in May 1, 1865.

Where mustered in Manchester, Va

Bounty paid $ 100; due $ 100

Where credited

Company to which assigned

Remarks:

Book mark: Maa 644-65

Paxton

(339) Copyist.

Muster Record of Private Samuel Jones
8th Connecticut Infantry

Only black men whose race had been enslaved and who were counted as only 3/5 of a person in the Constitution of the United States of America had to have special General Orders for them to serve in regiments other than the segregated ones. When looking at soldiers in the Arizona Territory, for instance, one finds some very ethnic names: [96]

Aaw Check Kum
Abiza, Jesus
Amoh Oh
Kuh Chu Voal
Mookaan, Am
Vis, Ek Kaal

Asians, Mexicans, and Native Americans had not been enslaved. Therefore, they were listed as all other Union soldiers were. That is, except for the blacks.

Another clue to the racial identity of black cooks and undercooks is where they had enlisted. If a cook in a Connecticut regiment had enlisted in Manchester, Virginia, or Morganzia, Louisiana, or if an undercook in an Illinois regiment had enlisted in Vicksburg, Mississippi, they most likely were "Col'd."[97] White southern men did not join the Union Army to be cooks, even though there were many white cooks. However, in Broadfoot's volumes, white soldiers are not identified as such.

Another racial clue can be their name. There are many men, both black and white, with the name of John Smith. However, a New Hampshire regimental cook whose name is Scipio Africanus [98] leaves little doubt as to his racial identification.

However, until records of each Union state have been searched thoroughly, the extent of the integration of white units during the Civil War cannot be accurately determined. Neither can the answer be given to the following question. *"What other roles did black men play other than that of cooks and undercooks?"* No General Orders had directly addressed that question.

A number of teamsters have been identified in this book, such as those in the 1st Alabama Cavalry. Their names were discovered by Glenda McWhirter Todd [(99)] while researching records of those southern white men ("Unionists") who had not served the Confederacy. However, on the subject of the other roles preformed by blacks in white regiments, much more research needs to be done.

A perhaps confusing situation arises for a modern day researcher upon seeing the terminology "black" as used in cavalry regiments. In today's terminology, "black" refers to a "person of color," an African American. However, that is not what it meant on the Civil War rosters. Rather, it was an abbreviation for blacksmith.[(100)] The names of black blacksmiths and farriers are not as easily isolated as are those of the black cooks and undercooks due to General Orders 323.

Just as the Rebels lacked respect for the fighting abilities of black soldiers, the Yankees also held the same sentiments. Consequently, the Union Army instead of using the blacks for "soldiering," used them for military support: heavy labor construction workers, drivers, cooks, spies, scouts, nurses, servants, stevedores, general laborers, and blacksmiths.

Many having been military laborers before the signing of the Emancipation Proclamation, they were not raw recruits. They had been on the front lines and knew what to expect. What the Union Army offered black men was a new way of living, even to being better clothed and fed than they had ever been before. The Army offered them a glimpse of what freedom would be like and that was the most powerful incentive of all for them to be ready to pay "the last full measure of devotion." [(101)]

CHAPTER VI

Southern Unionists

Another surprise for me was to learn that every southern state with the exception of South Carolina had formed Union regiments. Those units were composed of "Unionists," white men whose allegiance was not to the Confederacy. A number of those regiments enlisted "Col'd" cooks.

The reasons for the white southerners joining the Union varied. Generally, they were poor men not feeling compelled to join forces with the rich plantation owners whose wealth was determined by the number of slaves they possessed.

Others resented the forced Confederate conscription. The Conscription Act had been enacted by the Confederate Congress in April 1862. At first it had stated that all able-bodied men between the ages of eighteen and thirty-five were to serve in the military. Sometime later, however, the ages were changed to be between seventeen and fifty. [102]

One group of Unionists, called "Buffaloes," [102] were white North Carolina soldiers who chose to wear the blue uniform rather than the gray. For instance, at Plymouth, North Carolina, during the battle that took place 17-20 April 1864, Companies B and E of the 2nd Regiment North Carolina Infantry were present. They were men from nearby Bertie County, having deserted the Confederate army to join the Federals.

Other "Buffaloes" may have been die-hard Unionists who sincerely wanted to preserve the Union. Still others may have been lured by the tempting "greenbacks" being dangled in front of them by the Federals as Confederate currency rapidly became worthless due to the unchecked inflation. However, the majority of the men had just wanted to be able to remain close to their families so as to protect them from becoming destitute, having no food or any means by which to grow any with the men *in absentia.* [103]

Another regiment of Unionists was the 1st Alabama Cavalry organized mainly in 1862 in Corinth, Mississippi, and Memphis, Tennessee. Mostly men of the hills who were not slave owners, they, too, varied in their reasons for joining the Union Army; but primarily they joined because of the Confederate Conscription Act.

According to the historian of the 1st Alabama Cavalry, Glenda McWhirter Dodd,

"Before the war, the Unionists stated their ancestors came to this country looking for a place to worship as they pleased and America allowed them to do that. Then their grandfathers and other ancestors fought too hard and suffered too much fighting for this country during the Revolutionary War and they just could not turn their backs on the same country nor fire on "Old Glory," the Flag of their forefathers. They also stated they didn't want to fight against their southern neighbors but things became so hot they hid out in a cave, now known as the 'Rock House' for months, trying to keep from having to make a decision. Finally the Confederates found them and forced them to either join or be shot on the spot. Many went ahead and joined but just long enough to make their way to the Union lines and sign on with them. This was their reasoning for joining the Union Army." [104]

After discovering my work on the website of historian Bennie McCrae [105] whose research and knowledge concerning the black soldiers during the Civil War is extensive, Glenda Todd contacted me via e-mail. She provided me with information concerning sixteen black soldiers she had been surprised to discover on the roster of the 1st Alabama Cavalry.

Several had been teamsters, helping me to answer the question of whether the black soldiers in white regiments were allowed jobs other than cooks and undercooks. Although they had enlisted under General Orders 323, seemingly, some were used in other support roles, as well.

For instance, Amos McKinney/McKenna, a slave who enlisted in the 1st Alabama Cavalry in Corinth, Mississippi, served as an undercook. However, when mustered out in Huntsville, Alabama, he was listed as a teamster with the regimental Quartermaster. Isaac Roberts and Garland Terry both were enlisted as undercooks, too, but also worked as teamsters. **(106)**

Another job for the black soldiers was that of blacksmith, such as Joel Poole (Pool) who enlisted and was mustered in as a private in Co. E in Rome, Georgia.[(107)] To determine which of the blacksmiths identified in *Roster of Union Soldiers* had been men of color, a researcher would have to study carefully each of their records.

The question has been asked as to whether or not black soldiers in white regiments had been combatants. That answer is found in some pension applications. Joel Poole reported that he had sustained a slight gunshot wound to his left ankle during a battle at Monroe's Crossroads, North Carolina. [(108)] Richard West of the 103d Pennsylvania Infantry reported that he had been shot in the leg during the Battle of Plymouth, North Carolina. [(109)]

All of the various roles black soldiers may have played in battles are not known, but their presence in life threatening positions is known. Teamsters in particular were especially in harm's way during battles. Amos McKinney of the 1st Alabama Cavalry stated on his pension application that he had been shot below the left knee and sustained several wounds to his chest when his unit was advancing on the enemy. [(110)]

Simon Samuel West, another black teamster, was hospitalized due to a shell wound in his right leg. In later years he received an invalid pension until his death on 25 January 1927. Although he was buried in the Highland Park Cemetery in Warrensville near Cleveland, Ohio, his grave was not marked by a Union tombstone. Thanks to the recent interest of historian Glenda Todd, the grave of Simon West finally is being recognized as that of a Union soldier.

In her own words, *"I completed the government form to request a Union Tombstone for Samuel/Simon West and forwarded it to the director. David Mitchell is his name, and he signed off on it and submitted it to the government to have the stone engraved and sent to him for erection, which he did promptly."* **(111)** The United States Government will install veteran tombstones *gratis*.

On 31 May 2008 the following persons participated in the dedication of Simon West's new Union tombstone: Sandra Craighead, Black History genealogist from Cleveland; Captain Luther Norman, Boy Scouts of America, Cleveland, Ohio; Steffon Jones, Civil War Historian, Youngstown, Ohio; Bertram Floyd, Military Miniature Creation, Sheffield, Ohio; Dale Henry, Civil War re-enactor, Springfield, Ohio; and Frederick Smith, Civil War re-enactor, Youngstown, Ohio.

The color guard consisted of four members of Boy Scouts Troop 812 of the North Coast Ranger Academy of Cleveland, Ohio. Followed by the five re-enactors, they paraded to the site of the veiled tombstone of Private Simon West, 1st Alabama Cavalry, Co. M.

His obituary was read by Sandi Craighead, and his military history was read by Steffon Jones. Following a prayer, the re-enactors fired several rounds in a salute. After Fred Smith removed the black veil from the new tombstone, hats were removed as "Taps" sounded in the background. **(112)**

Simon West's brand new tombstone in 2008 is more visible proof of the hypothesis that I had made in 1998. ***If there had been one black soldier in a white regiment, then there may have been more.***

Tombstone of Private Simon West
1st Alabama Cavalry
Courtesy of Sandra Craighead and Glenda Todd

Rifle Salute for Private Simon West
Reenactors: Dale Henry, Bertram Floyd, Steffon Jones
Boy Scouts Troop 812 - North Coast Ranger Academy, Cleveland, Ohio
Courtesy of Sandra Craighead and Glenda Todd

Reenactors and Boy Scouts show their respect for
Private Simon West
Dale Henry, Bertram Floyd, Steffon Jones, Frederick Smith
Courtesy of Sandra Craighead and Glenda Todd

After Glenda Todd me about the 1st Alabama Cavalry of Unionists, I queried her about the lives of the veterans when they returned home after the war had ended. I did not imagine they would have been warmly received by their neighbors who had remained true to the Confederacy. That was indeed true.

In the words of Glenda Todd, "*There are of stories of atrocities committed by the CSA against the Unionists and their families that you wouldn't believe. If you are brave enough and have the stomach for it, read the story of Henry Tucker on the new website, it will make you sick at your stomach. He was also one of my ancestors.* [113]

By reading the information contained on the website for the 1st Alabama Cavalry, [114] one easily can discover just how much the southern Unionists were hated. They sacrificed much by serving on the side that won the acrimonious war. When those veterans returned home they found that for them the war was not over.

Thanks to our modern world of technology the stories of the brave Unionists, too, are now being circulated to the general public, many totally unaware of the fact that some white southern men had fought for the Union. Recently, a young "Civil War buff," upon learning about the Unionists from me, wanted to know why they would have wanted to serve with the Union. My answer was, of course, that she would have to read my book to find her answer.

CONCLUSION

The importance of the list of names presented in this book, even if incomplete, is threefold. First, it may stimulate further research to document black Union soldiers who served in primarily white regiments. I have only "opened the door" to a fact few persons knew before 1998. Hopefully, now as it becomes more widely known, someone in the near future will do a more in depth study of the black soldiers who served in white regiments. In this book I have provided some of the tools I used for my research. Like in the story of Hansel and Gretel, following the clues is the secret to success.

Second, the list will give credibility to some families who have been told, but who have no actual proof that their ancestors had served in the Union Army. The story was passed from generation to generation, but the families possess no written proof for those men. If they did serve, however, that proof can be found at the National Archives.

Not until viewing the movie "Glory" and/or reading the novel *Roots*, many black people had not been thinking much about their ancestors. For one reason, access to pertinent records had been denied them during the bitter years of "Jim Crow." The information I was able to locate in 1999, for instance, at the state library in Raleigh, N.C., would not have been available to me in the not so distant segregated past of this country.

Now that an interest in black genealogy has been ignited, families are searching for and finding their ancestors. Among them may be Civil War soldiers, all of whom should be remembered and honored.

Since 1998, descendants have been thrilled to travel from near and far just to see the names of their ancestors engraved on the wall surrounding the "Spirit of Freedom" Monument in Washington, D.C. One such person is my stepmother's niece,

Christine Patterson. She was in D.C. for business purposes, and so asked me to accompany her to the monument to locate the name of her great grandfather, Samuel J. Patterson. I was happy to accompany her, and we easily found his name in the 5th Massachusetts Cavalry.

Some descendants, however, will arrive at the monument only to be disappointed by not finding their ancestors' names there. Neither will they be able to find them listed in the Black Soldiers' Database, making them ask, "*Was the story passed from generation to generation in our family simply folklore*?"

Perhaps not, because instead of serving in the segregated black regiments, their ancestors may have served in white units, as mine had. Therefore, a list, even though incomplete, needed to be compiled for descendants. Otherwise those soldiers might have remained forgotten and unrecognized forever. I have presented in 2008 such a list to the African American Civil War Museum in celebration of the 10th anniversary of "Spirit of Freedom."

Interestingly, another surprise was there for me at the monument. Whose name did I discover? And serendipitously in the same regiment as Samuel J. Patterson? **Thomas Patience**, a soldier with the same unusual surname as my great grandfather's. Just who was he? Another question needing an answer.

Third, the list, hopefully, will convince the "nay-sayers" who insist that there had been no black soldiers serving in white regiments during the Civil War when descendants of soldiers like Private Crowder Pacien of the 103rd Pennsylvania Volunteers insist there were, especially when those descendants have enlistment, muster, pension, and/or discharge records as proof. Or perhaps they already know where a black veteran is buried with his name, regiment, and company carved on his headstone, and flanking it, perhaps a GAR stanchion and an American flag.

BLACK SOLDIERS ALPHABETIZED

NAME	REGIMENT		STATE	COMPANY
Abbott, Benjamin	95th	Infantry	IL	Co. H
Abernathy, Reuben	66th	Infantry	IN	Co. D
Abraham, James	91st	Infantry	NY	Co. H
Abraham, Sidney	1st	Cavalry	LA	Co. D
Adams, Henry	46th	Infantry	OH	Co. A
Adams, Jackson	29th	Infantry	IL	Co. C
Adams, James	18th	Infantry	MO	Co. F
Adams, John	2nd	Lt. Art'y.	MO	Btt'y I
Adams, William	160th	Infantry	NY	Co. K
Adkins, Frederick	91st	Infantry	NY	Co. F, K
Adkins, Jacob	52nd	Infantry	IL	Co. F
Adkins, Peter	133rd	Infantry	NY	Co. F, K
Africanus, Scipio	2nd	Infantry	NH	Co. G
Africanus, Scipio	12th	Infantry	NH	Co. I
Aikens, Ephriam	3rd	Cavalry	MI	Co. B
Albert, Prince	54th	Infantry	IL	Co. A
Alexander, George	62nd	Infantry	IL	Co. F
Alexander, George	1st	Infantry	KS	Co. B
Alexander, Noah	78th	Infantry	IL	Co. A
Alexander, Thomas	4th	Cavalry	WI	Co. H
Alfred, James	8th	Infantry	MO	Co. F
Alfred, John	14th	Cavalry	NY	Co. B
Allen, John	7th	Cavalry	IN	Co. D
Allen, Solomon	8th	Infantry	KS	Co. I
Allen, Washington	3rd	Cavalry	MA	Co. A
Allison, James	1st	Infantry	LA	Co. K
Alsbrook, Joseph	25th	Infantry	IL	Co. I
Alston, Isaac	4th	Cavalry	WI	Co. F
Amos, Charles	3rd	Cavalry	NJ	Co. C, M
Anders, Joseph H.	3rd	Cavalry	NJ	Co. A
Anderson, Alexander	8th	Infantry	IL	Co. C
Anderson, Bruce	142nd	Infantry	NY	Co. K Medal of Honor *
Anderson, Charles H.	59th	Infantry	IL	Co. B
Anderson, Charles	89th	Infantry	IL	Co. B
Anderson, David	98th	Infantry	NY	Co. F, A

Anderson, George	2nd	Cavalry	OH	Co. G
Anderson, George	6th	Infantry	CA	Co. B
Anderson, Jacob	1st	Cavalry	MO	Co. K
Anderson, Jacob	7th	Cavalry	MO	Co. I
Anderson, John	12th	Infantry	IL	
Anderson, Lewis	28th	Infantry	IL	Co. K
Anderson, Lewis	91st	Infantry	IL	Co. K
Anderson, Morris	72nd	Infantry	IL	Co. D
Anderson, Peter	34th	Infantry	IO	Co. K
Anderson, Thomas	3rd	Cavalry	NJ	Co. M
Anderson, William	3rd	Cavalry	NJ	Co. L
Andrews, Andrew	17th	Infantry	MA	Co. A
Andrews, Edmond	83rd	Infantry	IL	Co. F
Andrews, George	17th	Infantry	MA	Co. A
Andrews, Jerry	32nd	Infantry	OH	Co. E
Annon, Alfred	165th	Infantry	NY	Co. A
Anthony, Albert	4th	Cavalry	IL	Co. I
Anthony, Jasper	4th	Cavalry	IL	Co. B, I
Anthony, Jasper	12th	Cavalry	IL	Co. I
Anthony, William	106th	Infantry	OH	Co. C
Archy, Torian	42nd	Infantry	IL	Co. K
Armstad, Henry	1st	Infantry	KS	Co. F
Armstead, Albert	118th	Infantry	IL	Co. A
Armstead, Stark	9th	Infantry	IL	
Armstead, William M.	2nd	Cavalry	MN	
Armstead, Willis	52nd	Infantry	IL	Co. D
Armstrong, Ed	79th	Infantry	OH	Co. F
Arnold, Oliver	118th	Infantry	IL	Co. D
Aron, Marion	24th	Infantry	MO	Co. H
Arthur, John	11th	Infantry	MO	Co. B
Arthur, John	7th	Infantry	MO	Co. K
Ash, Reuben	8th	Infantry	IL	Co. C
Ashby, Joseph	3rd	Cavalry	OH	Co. H
Ashby, William	34th	Infantry	IO	Co. I
Ashby, William	38th	Infantry	IO	Co. B, I
Atkins, Hilliard	6th	Infantry	MO	Co. C
Atus, James	57th	Infantry	PA	
Augustus, Alfred	5th	Heavy Art'y	RI	Co. A
Augustus, London	5th	Heavy Art'y	RI	Co. A
Austin, Charles	1st	Infantry	LA	Co. K
Austin, Porter	28th	Infantry	IL	Co. G
Austin, Porter	91st	Infantry	IL	Co. H

Austin, Samuel	95th	Infantry	IL	Co. F
Ayers, Peter	105th	Infantry	IL	Co. D
Babbitt, Erastmus	3rd	Cavalry	TN	Co. A
Bachelor, Ned	1st	Lt. Art'y.	IL	Btt'y. D
Bailey, Charles	9th	Infantry	IL	Co. C
Bailey, Francis	4th	Cavalry	WI	Co. C
Bailey, Joseph	10th	Infantry	TN	Co. B
Bailey, Richard	83rd	Infantry	IL	Co. A
Baird, Berdant	16th	Heavy Art'y	NY	Co. K
Baker, John	18th	Infantry	MO	Co. C
Baker, Washington	124th	Infantry	IL	Co. H
Baldwin, Charles	124th	Infantry	IL	Co. K
Balentine, Henry	52nd	Infantry	IL	Co. K
Balfour, John M.	13th	Infantry	MI	Co. K
Ball, Edwin	132nd	Infantry	NY	Co. D
Ball, Edwin	99th	Infantry	NY	Co. K, A
Ball, John	21st	Infantry	MO	Co. H
Ballantine, Columbus	18th	Infantry	MO	Co. A
Ballard, David	155th	Infantry	NY	Co. E
Banes, Preston	1st	Lt. Art'y	IL	Btt'y B
Banks, Eli F.	1st	Cavalry	FL	Co. C
Banks, Richard	14th	Cavalry	IL	Co. I
Banks, Simon	74th	Infantry	OH	Co. C
Barber, Handy	66th	Infantry	IL	Co. B
Bards, John E.	102nd	Infantry	IL	Co. I
Barker, John	1st	Cavalry	FL	Co. D
Barkman, Peter	1st	Cavalry	LA	Co. A
Barnes, David	98th	Infantry	IL	Co. A
Barnes, Henry	118th	Infantry	IL	Co. H
Barnes, Sandy	2nd	Lt. Art'y.	IL	Btt'y C
Barnett, George	44th	Infantry	IN	Co. H
Barnett, John	3rd	Mtd. Infantry	NC	Co. B
Barney, Marcellus	15th	Infantry	ME	Co. B
Barrett, Isam	1st	Infantry	KS	Co. B
Barrow, David	133rd	Infantry	NY	Co. A
Barrow, Reuben	11th	Cavalry	MO	Co. F
Barzine, Solomon	81st	Infantry	IL	Co. D
Bass, Alfred	98th	Infantry	IL	Co. B
Bass, Henry	53rd	Infantry	IL	Co. K
Bass, Jesse	102nd	Infantry	IL	Co. K
Battie, Bird	105th	Infantry	IL	Co. G
Battie, Mat	105th	Infantry	IL	Co. G
Batties, John	159th	Infantry	NY	Co. E
Battle, Moses	55th	Infantry	IL	Co. C
Battuse, Henry	118th	Infantry	IL	Co. H

Name	No.	Branch	State	Unit
Bay, Lundy	81st	Infantry	IL	Co. K
Beal, William	162nd	Infantry	NY	Co. A
Bean, John	15th	Cavalry	IL	Co. G
Beard, Henry	105th	Infantry	IL	Co. A
Beasley, Brisber	102nd	Infantry	IL	Co. F
Beasley, Edward/Edmond	58th	Infantry	IL	Co. H, A
Beasley/Beazley, Charles	58th	Infantry	IL	Co. D
Bebly, Green	19th	Infantry	IL`	Co. F
Beck, Lewis		Lt. Art'y.	KS	3rd Ind. Btt'y.
Beck, Lewis		Lt. Art'y.	KS	2nd Ind. Btt'y.
Beck, Samuel	1st	Lt. Art'y.	MO	Btt'y K
Beck, Samuel		Lt. Art'y.	KS	2nd Ind. Btty.
Beck, Samuel		Lt. Art'y.	KS	3rd Ind. Btt'y.
Bedell, Bristol	124th	Infantry	IL	Co. C
Beecher, Henry W.	173rd	Infantry	NY	Co. I
Bell, Charles	65th	Infantry	IL	Co. G
Bell, Charles	56th	Infantry	IL	Co. F
Bell, Ellick	3rd	Cavalry	TN	Co. C
Bell, Enos	26th	Lt. Art'y.	OH	Indpt. Batt'y
Bell, Jacob	4th	Cavalry	IL	Co. C
Bell, Jacob	12th	Cavalry	IL	Co. L
Bell, Richard	3rd	Cavalry	TN	Co. H
Bell, Thomas	8th	Infantry	KS	Co. F
Bembine, John	118th	Infantry	IL	Co. F
Bennett, Joseph	56th	Infantry	MA	Co. B
Bennett, Tip	1st	Infantry	KS	Co. G
Bentley, Benjamin	4th	Cavalry	WI	Co. K
Benton, William H.	11th	Cavalry	MO	Co. G
Berg, Cleve	57th	Infantry	IL	Co. A
Berguin, Morris	176th	Infantry	NY	Co. G
Berry, Alexander	13th	Cavalry	IL	Co. A, K
Berry, Philip	34th	Infantry	IL	Co. F
Berry, Reuben	3rd	Cavalry	MI	Co. A
Berry, Thomas	129th	Infantry	IL	Co. E
Berry, Ward		Lt. Art'y.	KS	3rd Ind. Btt'y.
Betts, Samuel	90th	Infantry	NY	Co. K, A
Bibbins, Anthony	30th	Infantry	MA	Co. H
Bird, Benjamin	4th	Cavalry	IL	Co. A
Bird, Eldred	19th	Infantry	MI	Co. E
Bishop, Columbus	62nd	Infantry	IL	Co. K
Bisker/Basker, Henry	2nd	Infantry	NH	Co. D
Bisker/Basker, Henry	12th	Infantry	NH	Co. B
Black, Alfred	7th	Cavalry	IL	Co. G
Black, James	9th	Infantry	ME	Co. K
Black, Osker	7th	Cavalry	IL	Co. G

Blackbon, Jefferson	8th	Infantry	MO	Co. K
Blair, Abraham	12th	Cavalry	IL	Co. C
Blair, Lewis W.	10th	Infantry	IL	Co. H
Blair, Reuben	50th	Infantry	IL	Co. D
Blake, Domingo	8th	Infantry	ME	Co. E
Blakeman, Allen	21st	Infantry	MO	Co. I
Blandon, John	9th	Cavalry	OH	Co. H
Blow, Thomas	18th	Infantry	MO	Co. I
Blue, Archy	4th	Cavalry	WI	Co. G
Body, Isaac	3rd	Cavalry	MI	Co. H
Boiscoe, Mason	11th	Cavalry	MO	Co. C
Boiscoe, Mason	3rd	Cavalry	MO	Co. K, B
Bolen, John G.	2nd	Cavalry	IL	Co. A
Boles, Samuel	13th	Infantry	ME	Co. I
Boles, Samuel	30th	Infantry	ME	Co. I, A
Booker, Elisha	32nd	Infantry	OH	Co. H
Booker, Irving	118th	Infantry	IL	Co. B
Booker, James	8th	Infantry	MO	Co. A
Boone, Daniel	14th	Cavalry	KS	Co. G
Borain, Abram	95th	Infantry	IL	Co. G
Botts, William	3rd	Cavalry	CO	Co. E
Bowen, John	43rd	Infantry	IL	Co. K
Bowen, Manuel	43rd	Infantry	IL	Co. K
Bowman, Pompey	7th	Infantry	MO	Co. E
Boyd, Henry	95th	Infantry	IL	Co. G
Boyd, William	30th	Infantry	MO	Co. B
Boyl, Tobias (Tob)	8th	Infantry	IL	Co. I
Bracy, Charles	124th	Infantry	IL	Co. K
Braden, Porter	50th	Infantry	IL	Co. D
Braddy, Moses	1st	Infantry	NC	Co. G
Braden, Charles	1st Lt. Art'y		MI	Batt'y B
Bradford, Sandy	1st	Cavalry	CO	Co. G
Bradgett, Cagy	71st	Infantry	OH	Co. C
Bradley, Henry	1st	Cavalry	LA	Co. A
Braide, Alexander	110th	Infantry	NY	Co. K
Bramlet, Henry	66th	Infantry	IL	Co. K
Branch, John	105th	Infantry	IL	Co. F
Branch, John	105th	Infantry	IL	Co. F
Brannon, Moses	2nd	Cavalry	FL	Co. C
Brayden, Lymus	50th	Infantry	IL	Co. H
Breckenridge, Samuel	29th	Infantry	IL	Co. D
Brides, Mac	4th	Cavalry	WI	Co. F
Bridges, Cato	34th	Infantry	IL	
Brinden, George	11th	Cavalry	IL	Co. C
Brinkley, Simon	1st	Infantry	NC	Co. F

Briscoe, Emanuel	160th	Infantry	NY	Co. D
Brister, Charles	34th	Infantry	NJ	Co. A
Brister, Charles	82nd	Infantry	PA	Co. G
Bristol, George	58th	Infantry	IL	Co. A
Britton, William	2nd	Cavalry	IL	Co. K, B
Broocks, Wesley	8th	Infantry	MO	Co. K
Brooks, Charles	1st	Cavalry	CO	Co. G
Brooks, Jackson	72nd	Infantry	IL	Co. D
Brooks, Samuel	7th	Cavalry	MO	Co. K
Brooks, Thomas	8th	Infantry	VT	Co. K
Brothers, Tom	155th	Infantry	NY	Co. K
Brotten, John	8th	Infantry	MD	Co. K
Brown, Abram	91st	Infantry	NY	Co. G
Brown, Abram	159th	Infantry	NY	Co. C
Brown, Adam	159th	Infantry	NY	Co. G
Brown, Albert	56th	Infantry	IL	Co. B
Brown, Amos	156th	Infantry	NY	Co. C
Brown, Barney	5th	Infantry	MN	Co. A
Brown, Benjamin	1st	Cavalry	CO	Co. H, G
Brown, Bloomfield	51st	Infantry	NY	Co. A
Brown, Bloomfield	109th	Infantry	NY	Co. A
Brown, Charles	129th	Infantry	IL	Co. K
Brown, Dease	4th	Calvary	MA	Co. L
Brown, E.	74th	Infantry	IN	Co. A
Brown, Elias	44th	Infantry	IN	Co. A
Brown, Frank	7th	Cavalry	IL	Co. B
Brown, Frank	4th	Infantry	MI	Co. D
Brown, George	176th	Infantry	NY	Co. E
Brown, Henry	1st New Orleans Inf.		LA	Co. B
Brown, Henry	1st	Infantry	LA	Co. B
Brown, Isaac	7th	Cavalry	IN	Co. A, C
Brown, Isaac	72nd	Infantry	IL	Co. A
Brown, Jackson	1st	Cavalry	LA	Co. A
Brown, James	89th	Infantry	IL	Co. E
Brown, James	102nd	Infantry	NY	Co. A
Brown, James	109th	Infantry	NY	Co. D
Brown, James	1st	Cavalry	LA	Co. D
Brown, James	21st	Infantry	MO	Co. G
Brown, James	2nd	Lt. Art'y.	MO	Btt'y C
Brown, Jim	59th	Infantry	IL	Co. H
Brown, John	19th	Infantry	IL	Co. H
Brown, John	43rd	Infantry	IL	Co. E
Brown, John	50th	Infantry	IL	Co. K
Brown, John	60th	Infantry	IL	Co. E

Brown, John	14th	Cavalry	NY	Co. B
Brown, John	51st	Infantry	NY	Co. C, B
Brown, John	118th	Infantry	IL	Co. F
Brown, John	164th	Infantry	NY	Co. F, H
Brown, Joseph	4th	Infantry	MI	Co. D
Brown, Joseph	1st	Cavalry	LA	Co. C
Brown, Kirby	1st	Cavalry	LA	Co. G
Brown, Leighton	56th	Infantry	MA	Co. I
Brown, Milton	11th	Infantry	IL	Co. C
Brown, Mingo	1st	Infantry	NC	Co. B
Brown, Nat	11th	Cavalry	MO	Co. E
Brown, Parker	1st	Cavalry	LA	Co. E
Brown, Richard	91st	Infantry	NY	Co. C
Brown, Samuel	32nd	Infantry	OH	Co. H
Brown, Solomon	30th	Infantry	MA	Co. E
Brown, Thomas	11th	Infantry	IL	
Brown, William	4th	Cavalry	WI	Co. A
Brown, William	6th	Cavalry	MI	Co. C
Brown, William	129th	Infantry	IL	Co. G
Bryan, Aleck	72nd	Infantry	IL	Co. D
Bryan, Norman	116th	Infantry	NY	Co. I
Bryan, Norman	90th	Infantry	NY	Co. A
Bryder, Mac	4th	Cavalry	WI	Co. F
Bual, Jackson	32nd	Infantry	OH	Co. G
Bucey, Isan	7th	Cavalry	IL	Co. I
Buchanan, Adam	Lt. Art'y		AK	1st Batt'y
Buck, Amos	111th	Infantry	IL	Co. E
Buckner, David	2nd	Infantry	OH	Co. G
Bullard, Aaron	47th	Infantry	PA	Co. D
Bullard, John	47th	Infantry	PA	Co. D, J
Bullock, Major	92nd	Infantry	IL	Co. B
Bunck, Henry	178th	Infantry	NY	Co. B
Bunkley, Solomon	118th	Infantry	IL `	Co. G
Bunton, Milton	129th	Infantry	IL	Co. I
Burl, William	1st	Infantry	KS	Co. G
Burnett, Cage	2nd	Lt. Art'y.	MO	Btt'y M
Burnett, John	164th	Infantry	NY	Co. H
Burney, Benjamin	32nd	Infantry	OH	Co. F
Burns, William	2nd	Lt. Art'y	IL	Battery F
Burrebeina, John	118th	Infantry	IL	Co. C
Burrell, George	3rd	Cavalry	MI	Co. K
Bush, Charles	23rd	Infantry	MO	Co. F
Bute, Amos	48th	Infantry	IL	Co. K
Butler, Benjamin	12th	Infantry	IL	Co. C
Butler, Joseph	4th	Cavalry	WI	Co. E

Butler, Lewis	3rd	Infantry	MN	Co. I
Butler, William	3rd	Cavalry	MA	Co. I, E
Byers, James	24th	Infantry	MO	Co. G, D
Caesar, Julius	105th	Infantry	IL	Co. H
Caldwell, Amos	52nd	Infantry	IL	Co. D
Calhoun, Caleb	32nd	Infantry	MA	Co. A, K
Calvin, James	1st	Infantry	KS	Co. H
Calvin, John	31st	Infantry	MO	Co. D
Calvin, John	32nd	Infantry	MO	Co. A, E
Cambell, Marshall	92nd	Infantry	IL	Co. E
Camel, Jackson	128th	Infantry	NY	Co. A
Camel, William	56th	Infantry	IL	Co. E
Campbell, Cato	12th	Cavalry	IL	Co. L
Campbell/Cambell, Cato	4th	Cavalry	IL	Co. C
Cannon, Miles	78th	Infantry	IL	Co. H
Carey, Edmund	159th	Infantry	NY	Co. D, A
Carney, Greene	24th	Infantry	MO	Co. C
Carr, Edward	99th	Infantry	NY	Co. B
Carr, Edward	132nd	Infantry	NY	Co. I
Carr, Isaac	99th	Infantry	NY	Co. B
Carr, Isaac	132nd	Infantry	NY	Co. A
Carr, William	7th	Infantry	IL	Co. H
Carroll, ?	18th	Infantry	MI	Co. H
Carroll, Washington	12th	Infantry	IL	Co. B
Carter, Alexander	8th	Infantry	MO	Co. K
Carter, Charles	4th	Cavalry	WI	Co. A
Carter, Dave	1st Lt. Art'y. Battery		IL	Co. D
Carter, Edward	7th	Infantry	CT	Co. I
Carter, Jackson	93rd	Infantry	IL	Co. H
Carter, James	7th	Infantry	IL	Co. H
Carter, John	Union Light Guards	Cavalry	OH	
Carter, John	2nd	Lt. Art'y.	IL	Battery L
Carter, Peter	2nd	Cavalry	IL	Co. F, A
Carter, Simon	13th	Cavalry	TN	Co. E
Carthur, George	1st	Infantry	KS	Co. F
Cary, Thomas	118th	Infantry	IL	Co. K
Cate, Nicholas	4th	Cavalry	WI	Co. C
Chalk, William	155th	Infantry	NY	Co. D
Chambers, George	4th	Infantry	MN	Co. K
Chaplin, Moses	4th	Cavalry	MA	Co. K
Charlton, Robert	52nd	Infantry	IL	Co. G
Chatman, Amos	2nd	Cavalry	IL	Co. H, E
Chew, Henry	51st	Infantry	NY	Co. A
Chew, Henry	109th	Infantry	NY	Co. A
Childs, John	46th	Infantry	IL	Co. D

Chisholm, John	8th	Infantry	ME	Co. G
Christian, Watson	96th	Infantry	NY	Co. E
Claiborne (Claburn), Arthur	46th	Infantry	IL	Co. C
Clark, Berry	31st	Infantry	OH	Co. H
Clark, Charles	3rd	Calvary	OH	Co. B
Clark, Frank	3rd	Cavalry	MA	Co. C
Clark, George	17th	Infantry	IL	Co. F
Clark, James	129th	Infantry	IL	Co. C
Clark, John	4th	Cavalry	WI	Co. A
Clark, Josiah	31st	Infantry	OH	Co. H
Clark, Marshall	31st	Infantry	MO	Co. F
Clark, William	7th	Cavalry	PA	Co. G.
Clark, William	15th	Infantry	CT	Co. D
Clavey, John	11th	Cavalry	NY	Co. C
Clay, Henry	8th	Infantry	VT	Co. G
Clay, Henry	129th	Infantry	IL	Co. G
Clay, Henry	178th	Infantry	NY	Co. B
Clay, Henry	1st	Cavalry	LA	Co. F
Clay, Henry	1st	Infantry	KS	Co. G
Clemens, Samuel	7th	Cavalry	PA	Co. H
Clifton, Lindsey	4th	Cavalry	WI	Co. K
Clinton, Henry	West Eng. Reg. Volunteers		MO	Co. K
Cloud, Solomon	8th	Infantry	PA	Co. B
Cobb, William	28th	Infantry	PA	Co. B
Cohen, Perry	7th	Infantry	IL	Co. A, B
Cole, Frank	18th	Infantry	IL	Co. K
Coleman, Frederick	32nd	Infantry	OH	Co. H
Coleman, Lee	3rd	Cavalry	OH	Co. H
Coleman, Robert	3rd	Cavalry	OH	Co. C
Collem, Horace	7th	Calvary	IL	Co. K
Collins, Hanson	24th	Infantry	MO	Co. E
Collins, John	9th	Infantry	IL	Co. F
Collins, John	27th	Infantry	IL	Co. K
Collins, Thomas (Tom)	1st	Cavalry	KS	Co. K
Collins, Thomas	16th	Cavalry	KS	Co. G
Collins, William	3rd	Cavalry	MA	Co. F, E, M
Colman, Wyatt	124th	Infantry	IL	Co. C
Colson, Sampson	43rd	Infantry	IL	Co. F
Columbia, Albert	148th	Infantry	NY	Co. B
Colwell, Edmund	32nd	Infantry	OH	Co. A
Conel, John	27th	Infantry	MO	Co. H
Conor, Levi	148th	Infantry	NY	Co. B
Cook, Abraham	124th	Infantry	IL	Co. A
Cook, Eli	3rd	Cavalry	MA	Co. I
Cook, Frederick	8th	Infantry	CT	Co. F

Name	Regiment	Branch	State	Company
Cooper, Willis	7th	Cavalry	PA	Co. I
Copeland, Samuel	129th	Infantry	IL	Co A
Cordell, Lee	32nd	Infantry	OH	Co. D
Coward, Charles	34th	Infantry	NJ	Co. A
Cox, George	12th	Cavalry	NY	Co. E
Cox, John	1st	Infantry	NC	Co. C
Crackman, Patio	81st	Infantry	NY	Co. K
Cramer, William	1st St. Mil.	Cavalry	MO	Co. C
Crandall, Spencer	96th	Infantry	NY	Co. B
Crawford, David	Lt. Art'y		AK	1st Batt'y
Crawford, Richard	8th	Infantry	CA	Co. B
Crawford, Thomas	95th	Infantry	IL	Co. B
Crawford, William H.	Lt. Art'y		AK	1st Batt'y
Cregg, John	56th	Infantry	IL	Co. F
Crockett, Washington	7th	Cavalry	IL	Co. I
Crosby, Burton	18th	Infantry	MI	Co. A
Crow, William	148th	Infantry	NY	Co. B
Cupid, Lem	95th	Infantry	IL	Co. C
Custer, William	3rd	Infantry	MN	Co. G
Daniel, Michael	1st	Infantry	KS	Co. C
Daniel, Parish	21st	Infantry	MO	Co. I
Daniels, Harrison	2nd	Cavalry	NJ	Co. B
Danna, Charles	17th	Infantry	OH	Co. B
Darden, Jonas	1st	Cavalry	MA	Co. I
Darden, Jonas	4th	Cavalry	MA	Co. A, I
Dart, Thomas	9th	Infantry	MI	Co. H
Daurity, Samuel	50th	Infantry	IL	Co. F
David, Doctor	54th	Infantry	OH	Co. A
Davidson, Augustus	13th	Cavalry	IL	Co. D
Davidson, Tilton	46th	Infantry	IL	Co. K
Davis, Bird	1st	Cavalry	AL	Co. D
Davis, Charles	56th	Infantry	IL	Co. B
Davis, Doctor	21st	Infantry	MO	Co. I
Davis, Harry	95th	Infantry	IL	Co. I
Davis, James	1st	Cavalry	CO	Co. B, F
Davis, John	1st New Orleans Inf.		LA	Co. A
Davis, John	1st	Infantry	LA	Co. A
Davis, Joseph	1st	Infantry	LA	Co. D
Davis, King	45th	Infantry	NY	Co. B
Davis, Michael	155th	Infantry	NY	Co. B
Davis, Robert	3rd	Cavalry	NJ	Co. G
Davis, Robert	8th	Infantry	IL	Co. G
Davis, Samuel	2nd	Cavalry	CO	Co. K
Davis, William	3rd	Cavalry	NJ	Co. B
Davis, William	1st	Cavalry	AL	Co. M

Davisison, Syrous	3rd	Cavalry	MI	Co. A
Day, Alfred	3rd	Cavalry	PA	Co. G
Dean, David	2nd	Lt. Art'y.	MO	Btt'y K
Dease, Bram	1st	Cavalry	MA	Co. L
Dease, Bram	4th	Cavalry	MA	Co. L
Defoe, William	102nd	Infantry	IL	Co. F
Delaney, Henry	90th	Infantry	NY	Co. E
Delaney, Henry	116th	Infantry	NY	Co. A
Denman, Riley	7th	Infantry	IL	Co. H
Devall, Richard	2nd	Infantry	MD	Co. G
Dickens, Bill	30th	Infantry	IL	Co. A
Dickens, Cicero	46th	Infantry	IL	Co. A
Dickens, Joshua	2nd	Cavalry	IL	Co. H, E
Dickens, Stephen	92nd	Infantry	IL	Co. K
Dickens, William	117th	Infantry	IL	Co. I
Dickerson, Ruben	8th	Infantry	MO	Co. A
Dickings, Samuel	3rd	Cavalry	MI	Co. L
Dickson, Bryan	1st	Infantry	KS	Co. H
Diggs, Henry	90th	Infantry	NY	
Diggs, John	72nd	Infantry	IL	Co. A
Dillahunt, James 111th Infantry transferred to 48th Infantry IL				Co. I
Dillon, Isaac	72nd	Infantry	IL	Co. E
Dimon, Samuel	1st	Infantry	LA	Co. K
Dismuke, Jacob	102nd	Infantry	IL	Co. G
Dixon, Lock	32nd	Infantry	OH	Co. A
Dixon, Thomas	7th	Infantry	MO	Co. B
Dobson, Henry	99th	Infantry	NY	Co. A
Dobson, Henry	132nd	Infantry	NY	Co. D
Dodd, William	95th	Infantry	IL	Co. H
Dodget, Archibald	4th	Cavalry	WI	Co. E,
Dogue, Dennis	91st	Infantry	NY	Co. B
Dorsey, Charles	72nd	Infantry	IL	Co. I
Dorsey, Frank	2nd	Infantry	NH	Co. B, F;
Dorsey, Frank	10th	Infantry	NH	Co. G;
Dorsey, Frank	12th	Infantry	NH	Co. D
Dorsey, John H.	12th	Infantry	NH	Co. B
Dorsey, John H.(a.k.a. William)	2nd	Infantry	NH	Co. B
Dosier, Joseph	20th	Infantry	IL	Co. C
Dotson, Thomas	31st	Infantry	MA	Co. E
Dougherty, Isaac	156th	Infantry	NY	Co. C
Douglas, Daniel	129th	Infantry	IL	Co D
Douglas, John	129th	Infantry	IL	
Douglass, Hezekiah Ford	95th	Infantry	IL	Co. C
Dover, John	4th	Cavalry	IL	Co. E
Dow, Miller	1st	Infantry	KS	Co. C

Dowe, Hilliard	1st	Infantry	NC	Co. G
Doyle, Alex	4th	Cavalry	WI	Co. F
Dozier, Anthony	8th	Infantry	ME	Co. K
Drain, Robert	83rd	Infantry	IL	Co. I
Draiton, Govern E.	2nd	Cavalry	AK	Co. D
Driggins, Edmund/Edward	74th	Infantry	OH	Co. B
Driggins, Edmund/Edward	98th	Infantry	OH	Co. F
Driggins, Peter	74th	Infantry	OH	Co. K
Duncan, Alfred	19th	Infantry	MI	Co. H
Duncan, Harrison	19th	Infantry	MI	Co. H
Easer, Charles	99th	Infantry	NY	Co. C
East, George	3rd	Cavalry	MI	Co. B
Easton, Henry	182nd	Infantry	NY	Co. C
Eddie, Bob	1st	Engineers	NY	Co. H
Edwards, Alexander	2nd	Cavalry	CA	Co. A
Edwards, John	1st	Mtd. Rifles	NY	Co. C
Edwards, John	19th	Infantry	IL	Co. D
Edwards, John	60th	Infantry	IL	Co. E
Edwards, William	21st	Infantry	MO	Co. I
Elder, Robert	1st	Infantry	KS	Co. K
Elderkin, J. Russell	58th	Infantry	MA	Co. C
Elegant, George	62nd	Infantry	IL	Co. A
Elic, Frank	159th	Infantry	NY	Co. E
Elic, Roseborough	117th	Infantry	IL	Co. F
Elick, John	7th	Cavalry	PA	Co. D
Elliott, Thomas	96th	Infantry	NY	Co. K
Ellis, Henry	46th	Infantry	IL	
Ellis, Hilliard	155th	Infantry	NY	Co. F
Ellison, Gansy	46th	Infantry	IL	Co. C
Ellix, Thomas L.	1st	Cavalry	CO	Co. G
Ely, Joseph	1st	Infantry	LA	Co. G
Emil, Victor	133rd	Infantry	NY	Co. F
Emmet, Robert	4th	Cavalry	WI	Co. K
Ennis, Richard	109th	Infantry	NY	Co. C
Epps, James	176th	Infantry	NY	Co. K
Evans, Benjamin	1st	Hvy. Art'y.	MN	Co. E
Evans, Clem	22nd	Cavalry	NY	Co. H
Evans, Harry/Henry	18th	Infantry	MO	Co. K
Evans, James	6th	Cavalry	MO	Co. G
Evans, Richard	3rd	Cavalry	MA	Co. C
Ewing, Fleming	11th	Cavalry	KS	Co. B
Fall, George	Lt. Art'y.		NY	24th Ind. Batt'y
Farley, Alfred	13th	Infantry	ME	Co. C
Farley, Alfred	30th	Infantry	ME	Co. K
Farmer (Forman), Simon	1st	Cavalry	AL	Co. A

Name	Regiment	Branch	State	Company
Farris, Henry	8th	Infantry	KS	Co. H
Faulis, Henry	102nd	Infantry	IL	Co. A
Faultner, Louis	3rd	Infantry	MN	Co. D
Feelin, Harrison	118th	Infantry	IL	Co. E
Ferguson, Matthew	95th	Infantry	IL	Co. H
Ficklin, Gabriel	1st	Cavalry	CO	Co. B, E
Fields, January	8th	Infantry	ME	Co. E
Fields, John	2nd	Cavalry	IL	Co. F, A
Fifer, Joseph	59th	Infantry	IL	Co. E
Fisher, Benjamin	34th	Infantry	NJ	Co. H
Fisher, William	15th	Cavalry	PA	Co. H
Fisher, Wyatt	105th	Infantry	IL	Co. K
Fitzgerald, John	72nd	Infantry	IL	Co. C
Flack, John	59th	Infantry	IL	
Flack, Tom	59th	Infantry	IL	Co. H
Flake, George	111th Infantry transferred to 48th		IL	Co. I
Flander, Samuel	55th	Infantry	PA	Co. K
Fletcher, Samuel	174th	Infantry	NY	Co. G
Floyd, Louis	57th	Infantry	IL	Co. E
Floyd, Rush	1st	Cavalry	MO	Co. D
Floyd, Rush	7th	Cavalry	MO	Co. D
Folk, Thomas	11th	Cavalry	PA	Co. M
Forbes, George	12th	Infantry	CT	Co. A
Forman, William	3rd	Cavalry	NJ	Co. L
Forrest, Frank	8th	Infantry	NH	Co. C
Foster, Haywood	66th	Infantry	IL	Co. A
Fox, William Dudley	2nd	Cavalry	MI	Co. F
Fox, William	173rd	Infantry	NY	Co. A
Frances, Peter	4th	Cavalry	WI	Co. D
Francis, Henry C.	6th	Infantry	CA	Co. B
Franklin, Benjamin D.	72nd	Infantry	IL	Co. A
Franklin, Benjamin	54th	Infantry	IL	Co. G
Franklin, William	129th	Infantry	IL`	Co. A
Freeman, George E.	14th	Hvy. Artillery	NY	Co. E
Freeman, George	103rd	Infantry	PA	Co. I
Frost, Henry	1st	Cavalry	LA	Co. G
Furguson, Edmond	83rd	Infantry	IL	Co. B
Furguson, Jim	8th	Infantry	ME	Co. D
Gabriel, Benjamin	1st	Infantry	KS	Co. F
Gabriel, Eli	50th	Infantry	IL	Co. I
Gaines, Andrew	14th	Cavalry	KS	Co. C
Gale, Sam	4th	Cavalry	WI	Co. G
Gardner, Cleveland	40th	Infantry	IL	
Gardner, Cleveland	93rd	Infantry	IL	Co. E
Garrett, Dolphus	103rd	Infantry	PA	Co. K

Garvine, Samuel	17th	Infantry	OH	Co. K
Gay, Freeman	17th	Infantry	OH	Co. C
Gayton, Peter	4th	Cavalry	WI	Co. G
Gazaphall, Franklin	2nd	Cavalry	IL	Co. K, B
George, James	13th	Infantry	ME	Co. K
George, James	30th	Infantry	ME	Co. K
Germany, John	4th	Cavalry	WI	Co. G
Gibbins, Gabiel	8th	Infantry	ME	Co. I
Gibbons, Carroll	1st	Infantry	KS	Co. H
Gibbons, Riley	1st	Infantry	KS	Co. H
Gibson, Piahmond	1st	Infantry	KS	Co, A, B
Gibson, Saunders	57th	Infantry	IL	Co. K
Gidwell, Jack	129th	Infantry	IL	Co. E
Gilmore, Austin	111th	Infantry	IL	Co. E
Giton, Henry	1st	Infantry	KS	Co. K
Glasgow, George	3rd	Cavalry	NJ	Co. F
Glover, Adam	18th	Cavalry	NY	Co. C, H
Godfrey, James	1st	Cavalry	MA	Co. I
Golding, Berry	30th	Infantry	MA	Co. F
Golson, Samuel	83rd	Infantry	IL	Co. B
Goodman, Richard S.	105th	Infantry	IL	Co. C
Gordon, Cleveland	40th	Infantry	IL	Co. K
Gordon, James	124th	Infantry	IL	Co. D
Gordon, William	30th	Infantry	IL	Co. K
Gordon, William	46th	Infantry	IL	Co. K
Gould, William	124th	Infantry	IL	Co. G
Graffell, Charles	2nd	Cavalry	CA	Co. H
Graham, Antoine	4th	Cavalry	WI	Co. E
Graham, David	7th	Cavalry	PA	Co. M
Graham, Harrison	8th	Infantry	KS	Co. F
Graham, Jefferson	128th	Infantry	NY	Co. D
Graham, Jefferson	144th	Infantry	NY	
Graham, Torey	1st	Infantry	NC	Co. L
Grant, Charles	2nd	Cavalry	IL	Co. F, A
Grant, Jacob	8th	Infantry	ME	Co. F
Grant, Joseph	8th	Infantry	ME	Co. G
Granville, Jack	3rd	Infantry	MN	Co. C
Granville, Samuel	103rd	Infantry	PA	Co. B
Grate, Mark	8th	Infantry	ME	Co. E
Gray, Milton	10th	Cavalry	MO	Co. C
Greeley, Horace	173rd	Infantry	NY	Co. I
Greeley, John	90th	Infantry	NY	Co. F
Greeley, John	116th	Infantry	NY	Co. E
Green, Boulon	118th	Infantry	IL	Co. I
Green, Burch	7th	Infantry	MO	Co. D

Green, Cook	11th	Infantry	IL	Co. E
Green, Frank	13th	Cavalry	IL	Co. D
Green, Gordon	78th	Infantry	IL	Co. F
Green, Henry	3rd	Cavalry	MA	Co G
Green, Isum	8th	Infantry	IL	Co. B
Green, James	56th	Infantry	IL	Co. E
Green, James	161st	Infantry	NY	Co. C
Green, John	11th	Cavalry	IL	Co. E
Green, John	43rd	Infantry	IL	Co. E
Green, John	7th	Infantry	MO	Co. D
Green, Lyman	8th	Infantry	ME	Co. G
Green, Moses	160th	Infantry	NY	Co. I
Green, Nat	13th	Infantry	ME	Co. F
Green, Robert	81st	Infantry	IL	Co. G
Green, Samuel	51st	Infantry	NY	Co. I
Gregor, William	1st	Infantry	KS	Co. H
Griffin, Bald	14th	Cavalry	NY	Co. B
Griffin, Charles P	18th	Cavalry	NY	Co. C
Griffin, George	18th	Infantry	NY	Co. A
Griffin, George	182nd	Infantry	NY	Co. C
Griffin, Monroe	10th	Infantry	MO	Co. D
Grigsby, Martin	9th	Infantry	IL	Co. H
Grisby, Charles	45th	Infantry	IL	Co. A
Grixby, Burk/Buck	9th	Infantry	IL	Co. F
Grummell, Samuel	59th	Infantry	IL	Co. A
Gunn, George W.	12th	Infantry	NH	Co. A
Guy, Benjamin	16th	Infantry	MI	Co. F
Guyan, John	14th	Hvy. Art'y.	NY	Co. A
Hagerman, Aaron	3rd	Cavalry	NJ	Co. G
Haines, David	3rd	Cavalry	MA	Co. F
Hall, Benjamin	176th	Infantry	NY	Co. D
Hall, Benjamin	1st	Cavalry	LA	Co. F
Hall, Caesar	3rd	Mounted Infantry	TN	Co. B
Hall, Charley	118th	Infantry	IL	Co. B
Hall, Martin	50th	Infantry	IL	Co. I
Hall, William	19th	Infantry	MI	Co. I
Halsey, John	3rd	Cavalry	MA	Co. L, D, K
Hamilton, Abraham	8th	Infantry	ME	Co. F
Hamilton, Henry	12th	Infantry	IL	Co. G
Handerson, Leffert	43rd	Infantry	IL	Co. E
Hanley, Fred	62nd	Infantry	IL	Co. B
Hanner, Samuel	50th	Infantry	IL	Co. D
Hanson, Bristol	58th	Infantry	IL	Co. F
Harden, William	1st	Lt. Art'y	MI	Batt'y B
Hardy (McRae), Titus	103rd	Infantry	PA	Co. K

Name	Regiment	Branch	State	Company
Hardy, Henry	56th	Infantry	IL	Co. D
Hardy, Tony	8th	Lt. Art'y.	NY	Ind. Batt'y
Hargraves, Joseph	148th	Infantry	NY	Co. A
Harmon, Simon	81st	Infantry	IL	Co. A
Harper, John	129th	Infantry	IL	Co. F
Harper, Jordan	129th	Infantry	IL	Co. F
Harper, Samuel	90th	Infantry	NY	Co. B
Harris, James	1st	Cavalry	MO	Co. H
Harris, L.	8th	Infantry	MD	Co. K
Harris, Robert	19th	Infantry	IL	Co. D
Harris, Robert	60th	Infantry	IL	Co. A
Harrison, Feelen	118th	Infantry	IL	Co. B
Harrison, George	38th	Infantry	MA	Co. C
Harrison, Henry	31st	Infantry	MA	Co. F, H, D
Harrison, William H.	90th	Infantry	NY	Co. B
Harrison, William Henry	19th	Infantry	IL	Co. A
Harrison, William	72nd	Infantry	IL	Co. G, H
Harvel, Richard	79th	Infantry	IL	
Harwood, John G.	18th	Infantry	IL	Co. B
Hasty, James	56th	Infantry	IL	Co. D
Haupt, Henry	31st	Infantry	MA	Co. G
Hawkins, Coleman	3rd	Infantry	MN	Co. E
Hawkins, Henry	8th	Infantry	NH	Co. C
Hayes, Caroll	54th	Infantry	IL	Co. H
Hays, George	1st	Cavalry	LA	Co. A
Hays, Joseph	3rd	Infantry	MN	Co. C
Hays, Smith	72nd	Infantry	IL	Co. C
Hayward, Bristol	8th	Infantry	ME	Co. F
Haywood, Frank	18th	Cavalry	NY	Co. E
Haywood, John	12th	Cavalry	NY	Co. L
Hazard, Robert	32nd	Infantry	OH	Co. A
Hazen, Samuel	176th	Infantry	NY	Co. I
Hemings, William Beverly	73rd	Infantry	OH	Co. H
Hemings, Thomas Eston	175th	Infantry	OH	Co. E
Hemperton, John	1st	Infantry	KS	Co. I
Henderson, Benjamin	13th	Infantry	ME	Co. B
Henderson, Benjamin	30th	Infantry	ME	Co. H
Henderson, Beverly	25th	Infantry	OH	Co. K
Henderson, Beverly	107th	Infantry	OH	Co. D
Henderson, James	4th	Cavalry	IL	Co. B
Henderson, James	12th	Cavalry	IL	Co. I
Henderson, Thomas	12th	Infantry	IL	Co. E
Henderson, Thomas	72nd	Infantry	IL	Co. E
Henderson, Thomas	182nd	Infantry	NY	Co. I
Henderson, William	26th	Infantry	MA	Co. B

Henderson, William	38th	Infantry	MA	Co. D
Henman, James	1st	Infantry	KS	
Henry, John	8th	Infantry	VT	Co. G
Henry, Peter	9th	Infantry	MI	Co. G
Henry, William	5th	Heavy Art'y	RI	Co. K
Henry, William	57th	Infantry	OH	Co. B
Henry, William	98th	Infantry	NY	Co. C
Herd, John	46th	Infantry	IL	Co. D
Herdy Riley	12th	Cavalry	IL	Co. I
Herdy, Riley	4th	Cavalry	IL	Co. B
Herron, Benjamin	83rd	Infantry	IL	Co. I
Hestel, Samuel	10th	Cavalry	MO	Co. K
Hester, John	16th	Cavalry	KS	Co. G
Hester, John	1st	Infantry	KS	Co. B
Hickman, James	7th	Cavalry	PA	Co. C
Hicks, John	2nd	Cavalry	IL	Co. I
Hicks, William	21st	Infantry	MO	Co. F
Higden, Andrew	50th	Infantry	IL	Co. K
Hill, Ely	43rd	Infantry	IL	Co. D
Hill, Green T.	66th	Infantry	IL	Co. D
Hill, James	4th	Cavalry	IL	Co. A
Hill, Joseph	18th	Infantry	MI	Co. H
Hill, Morgan	18th	Infantry	MI	Co. D
Hilliard, Dick	95th	Infantry	IL	Co. F
Hilliard, Jackson	1st	Cavalry	LA	Co. A
Hines, Richard	15th	Infantry	ME	Co. B
Hobson, Mike	124th	Infantry	IL	Co. I
Hogan, Alexander	10th	Infantry	IL	Co. H
Hollin, Humphry	99th	Infantry	NY	Co. B
Hollin, Humphry	175th	Infantry	NY	Co. A
Holly George	81st	Infantry	IL	Co. B
Holmes, Charles	82nd	Infantry	PA	Co. G
Holmes, Daniel	7th	Cavalry	PA	Co. I
Holmes, Daniel	4th	Cavalry	WI	Co. A,
Holmes, James H.	34th	Infantry	NJ	Co. B
Holt, Bucker	26th	Infantry	MO	Co. D
Horton, Wiliford	1st	Cavalry	FL	Co. C
Horton, William R.	3rd	Mtd. Infantry	NC	Co. I
Hours, Merret	13th	Cavalry	TN	
Houston, Martin	11th	Infantry	IL	Co. H
Howard, George	30th	Infantry	NY	Co. D
Howard, Jeremiah	108th	Infantry	NY	Co. A
Howard, Lot	57th	Infantry	IL	Co. B
Howes, Benjamin	32nd	Infantry	OH	Co. G
Hubbard, Guttrill	8th	Infantry	IL	Co. A

Hudson, Gabe	46th	Infantry	IL	Co. H	
Hudson, Gilbert	118th	Infantry	IL	Co. A	
Hudson, Joshua	46th	Infantry	IL	Co. H	
Hudson, Peter	51st	Infantry	IL	Co. E	
Hugh, John	8th	Infantry	ME	Co. C	
Hughes, Green	2nd	Cavalry	CO	Co. K	
Hunt, Nelson	25th	Infantry	MO		
Hunter, Robert	21st	Infantry	MO	Co. A	
Hurdel, Wesley	3rd Lt. Art'y.		NY	Batt'y	Co. K
Hurt, Richard	8th	Infantry	IL	Co. B	
Hurt, Richard	17th	Infantry	IL	Co. C	
Hurt, William	21st	Infantry	MO	Co. D	
Huston, Andrew	66th	Infantry	IL	Co. D	
Hutchinson, James	8th	Infantry	CA	Co. B	
Huzen, Simon	12th	Cavalry	NY	Co. I	
Hye, Thomas	89th	Infantry	OH	Co. I	
Ingam, Daniel	18th	Infantry	IL	Co. I	
Isaac, James	182nd	Infantry	NY	Co. B	
Jack, Christopher	118th	Infantry	IL	Co. E	
Jackson, Aaron	90th	Infantry	NY	Co. C	
Jackson, Aaron	133rd	Infantry	NY	Co. K	
Jackson, Alexander	156th	Infantry	NY	Co. I	
Jackson, Andrew	1st	Cavalry	TX	Co. E	
Jackson, Andrew	160th	Infantry	NY	Co. E	
Jackson, Andrew	8th	Infantry	KS	Co. H	
Jackson, Charles	12th	Infantry	IL	Co. H	
Jackson, Charles	1st New Orleans Inf.		LA	Co. D	
Jackson, Charles	1st	Infantry	LA	Co. I	
Jackson, Edward	31st	Infantry	MA	Co. K	
Jackson, Isaac	1st	Cavalry	LA	Co. A	
Jackson, Jerry	72nd	Infantry	IL	Co. D	
Jackson, John H.	175th	Infantry	NY	Co. C	
Jackson, John	32nd	Infantry	OH	Co. D	
Jackson, Matthew	102nd	Infantry	IL	Co. B	
Jackson, Peter	Vet. Infantry 1st Batt'n		NJ	Co. B	
Jackson, Peter	1st	Infantry	NJ	Co. K	
Jackson, Samuel	14th	Infantry	NY	Co. M	
Jackson, Samuel	1st	Cavalry	ME	Co. F	
Jackson, Thomas	9th	Infantry	CT	Co. F	
Jackson, William	7th	Infantry	IL	Co. B	
Jacobs, Abram	18th	Infantry	IL	Co. G	
James, Frank	14th	Cavalry	NY	Co. C	
James, Frank	18th	Cavalry	NY	Co. C	
James, John	60th	Infantry	IL	Co. F	
Jefferson, Albert	10th	Infantry	IL	Co. B	

Jefferson, Beverly (Hemings) 1st Infantry WI Co. E
Jefferson, John Wayles (Hemings) 8th Infantry WI Colonel
Jefferson, Horace 45th Infantry IL Co. K
Jefferson, Joseph 165th Infantry NY Co. D
Jefferson, Thomas 4th Cavalry WI Co. H
Jefferson, Thomas 155th Infantry NY Co. G
Jefferson, Thomas 164th Infantry NY Co. C
Jenkins, John 8th Infantry ME Co. D
Jenkins, Josiah 173rd Infantry NY Co. E
Jenkins, Philip``` 160th Infantry NY Co. B
Jenkins, Stephen 8th Infantry ME Co. D
Jennings, Richard 111th Infantry transferred to 48th IL Co. H
Johnson, Albert 102nd Infantry IL Co. C
Johnson, Alec 85th Infantry NY
Johnson, Augustus 4th Cavalry IL Co. C
Johnson, Bill 58th Infantry IL Co. B
Johnson, Blunt 176th Infantry NY Co. B
Johnson, Cornelius 182nd Infantry NY Co. C, E
Johnson, Felix 40th Infantry IL Co. K
Johnson, Francis 45th Infantry NY Co. F
Johnson, Frederick 174th Infantry NY Co. H
Johnson, Frederick 162nd Infantry NY Co. H
Johnson, Harrison 1st Cavalry NE Co. H
Johnson, Harry 11th Cavalry MO Co. D
Johnson, Henry 160th Infantry NY Co. B
Johnson, Henry 3rd Cavalry NJ Co. H
Johnson, Henry 101st Infantry PA Co. C
Johnson, Henry 155th Infantry NY Co. C
Johnson, Henry 1st New Orleans Inf. LA Co. C
Johnson, Henry 1st Infantry LA Co. C
Johnson, Israel 91st Infantry NY Co. A
Johnson, Jacob 8th Infantry ME Co. A
Johnson, Joe 4th Infantry MN Co. G
Johnson, John 1st New Orleans Inf. LA Co. H
Johnson, John 1st Infantry LA Co. I
Johnson, Jordan 77th Infantry IL Co. C
Johnson, Joseph 124th Infantry IL Co. B
Johnson, Josiah 90th Infantry NY Co. D
Johnson, Lawrence 178th Infantry NY Co. D
Johnson, Oliver 8th Infantry CT Co. I
Johnson, Peter 38th Infantry IO Co. K
Johnson, Richard 14th Cavalry NY Co. A
Johnson, Samuel 21st Infantry MO Co. C
Johnson, Spencer 4th Cavalry WI Co. H
Johnson, Spenser 4th Cavalry WI Co. H

Johnson, Thomas	29th	Infantry	IL	Co. C
Johnson, Thomas	1st	Cavalry	LA	Co. A
Johnson, William H.	2nd	Infantry	CT	
Johnson, William Henry	8th	Infantry	CT	
Johnson, William	51st	Infantry	IL	Co. E
Johnson, William	34th	Infantry	NJ	Co. E
Johnson, William	178th	Infantry	NY	Co. D
Johnson, William	21st	Infantry	MO	Co. F
Johnston, Augustus	12th	Cavalry	IL	Co. L
Johnston, George	1st	Infantry	KS	Co. E
Johnston, John	155th	Infantry	NY	Co. C
Johnston, Overton	160th	Infantry	NY	Co. C
Johnston, Peter	182nd	Infantry	NY	Co. I
Jonas, Aaron	99th	Infantry	NY	Co. A
Jonas, Aaron	132nd	Infantry	NY	Co. G
Jones, Adam	165th	Infantry	NY	Co. A
Jones, Amos	6th	Cavalry	MO	Co. E
Jones, Andrew	164th	Infantry	NY	Co. H
Jones, Benjamin	116th	Infantry	NY	Co. G
Jones, Cato	31st	Infantry	OH	Co. K
Jones, Dick	1st	Infantry	KS	Co. C
Jones, Eli	74th	Infantry	IN	Co. I
Jones, Eli	22nd	Infantry	IN	Co. D
Jones, Elias	82nd	Infantry	IN	Co. D
Jones, Elias	118th	Infantry	IL	Co. D
Jones, Frank	66th	Infantry	IN	Co. I
Jones, George	4th	Cavalry	IL	Co. C
Jones, George	12th	Cavalry	IL	Co. L
Jones, George	82nd	Infantry	IN	Co. G
Jones, George	11th	Cavalry	MO	Co. D
Jones, Green	22nd	Infantry	IN	Co. E
Jones, Green	82nd	Infantry	IN	Co C
Jones, Henry	27th	Cavalry	NY	Co. G
Jones, Henry	98th	Infantry	NY	Co. I
Jones, James	19th	Cavalry	PA	
Jones, James	62nd	Infantry	IL	Co. F
Jones, Jerry	21st	Infantry	MO	Co. A
Jones, Jordan	72nd	Infantry	IL	Co. G
Jones, Lucien	62nd	Infantry	IL	Co. B
Jones, Matthew	1st	Cavalry	FL	Co. E
Jones, Nat	4th	Cavalry	IL	Co. B
Jones, Paul	30th	Infantry	IL	Co. C
Jones, Peter	176th	Infantry	NY	Co. H
Jones, Richard	1st	Cavalry	FL	Co. F
Jones, Robert	105th	Infantry	IL	Co. D

Jones, Samuel	8th	Infantry	CT	Co. A
Jones, Samuel	161st	Infantry	NY	Co. C
Jones, Scipio	90th	Infantry	NY	Co. E
Jones, Spencer	4th	Cavalry	WI	Co. A
Jones, Stephen	95th	Infantry	IL	Co. C
Jones, Thomas	28th	Infantry	IL	Co. A
Jones, Thomas	110th	Infantry	NY	Co. I
Jones, Toney	90th	Infantry	NY	Co. A
Jones, William	19th	Infantry	IL	Co. D
Jones, William	178th	Infantry	NY	Co. D
Jones, Willis	15th	Cavalry	KS	Co. B
Kealin, Benjamin	6th	Infantry	MO	Co. H
Kelly, Henry	95th	Infantry	IL	Co. E
Kelly, William	4th	Cavalry	WI	Co. C
Kerson, Daniel	182nd	Infantry	NY	Co. H
Kimbeau, James	57th	Infantry	OH	Co. B
Kimmens, Elijah	4th	Infantry	MN	Co. A
King, Davis	58th	Infantry	NY	Co. B
King, Henry	48th	Infantry	IL	Co. D
King, Joseph	1st New Orleans Inf.		LA	Co. E
King, Joseph	1st	Infantry	LA	Co. H
Knight, Jacob	155th	Infantry	NY	Co. E
Knowles, Henry	4th	Cavalry	IL	Co. A
Knowles, John	3rd	Infantry	MN	Co. F
Lajenne, John Lewis	8th	Infantry	CA	Co. D
Lalter, Jordan	1st	Infantry	KS	Co. B
Lamar, Peter	15th	Cavalry	IL	Co. B
Lambert, William H.	2nd	Cavalry	CA	Co. D
Lane, Dick	Lt. Art'y.		MN	1st Ind. Batt'y
Lane, Stephen	11th	Cavalry	KS	Co. K
Langley, George W.	11th	Cavalry	PA	Co. A
Laterfield (Satterfield), Louis	4th	Cavalry	WI	Co. B
Latham, Simon	98th	Infantry	NY	Co. E
Lathrum, Henry	1st Lt. Art'y		MI	Batt'y H
Lee, Buck	66th	Infantry	IL	Co. H
Lee, Edward	7th	Cavalry	PA	Co. L
Lee, Elisha or Elias	155th	Infantry	NY	Co. I
Lee, Henry	72nd	Infantry	IL	Co. I
Lee, James A.	11th	Cavalry	KS	Co. M
Lee, James	118th	Infantry	IL	Co. E
Lee, Lucius	2nd	Infantry	NH	Co. E
Lee, Lucius	12th	Infantry	NH	Co. C
Lee, William	26th	Infantry	MA	
Lee, Wilson	38th	Infantry	MA	Co. E
Legree, Richard	8th	Infantry	ME	Co. K

Lemmon, William	3rd	Cavalry	NJ	Co. I
Leonard, Sam	4th	Cavalry	WI	Co. G
Lett, Aquilla	13th	Infantry	MI	Co. K
Leverett, Carolina	1st	Engineers	NY	Co. H
Levi, Antoine	162nd	Infantry	NY	Co. H
Levi, George	109th	Infantry	NY	
Levi, Henry	90th	Infantry	NY	Co. K, A
Lewis, Charles	6th	Infantry	MO	Co. I
Lewis, Emanuel	57th	Infantry	IL	Co. K
Lewis, Noah	5th	Heavy Art'y	RI	Co. F
Lewis, Samuel	1st	Cavalry	MO	Co. L
Lewis, Samuel	7th	Cavalry	MO	Co. G
Lewis, Timothy	1st	Infantry	NC	Co. H
Lewis, William	8th	Infantry	ME	Co. B
Lightfoot, Benjamin	18th	Infantry	IL	Co. E
Lightfoot, Marion	54th	Infantry	IL	Co. G
Link, Robert	105th	Infantry	IL	Co. B
Locklin, Erastus M.	1st	Cavalry	FL	Hospital
Lodge, Charles	1st	Infantry	NC	Co. E
Lomax, Andrew	14th	Cavalry	NY	Co. M
Long, Benjamin	98th	Infantry	NY	Co. D
Long, Jerry	12th	Infantry	IL	Co. I
Long, William	12th	Infantry	IL	Co. G
Lucas, John	81st	Infantry	IL	Co. C
Lunda, Bay	50th	Infantry	IL	Co. K
Lymus, Brayden	50th	Infantry	IL	Co. H
MacDryfuss, Shelby	7th	Cavalry	PA	Co. F
Mack, Ed	2nd	Cavalry	IL	Co. I
Mack, James	4th	Cavalry	WI	Co. L
Mack, James	161st	Infantry	NY	Co. I
Mackey, Henry	58th	Infantry	PA	Co. G
Mackey, Joseph	165th	Infantry	NY	Co. E
Maddox, George	1st Bn.	Cavalry	NV	Co. B
Madison, Coriolanus	24th	Infantry	IL	Co. A
Maguire, George	129th	Infantry	IL	Co. I
Malvin, Robert	124th	Infantry	IL	Co. G
Manningcar, Addison	57th	Infantry	IL	Co. E
Marcus, Frank	31st	Infantry	MA	Co. B, A, K
Mars, Frank	54th	Infantry	IL	Co. A
Marshall, John	27th	Infantry	MO	Co. H
Martin, Alexander	155th	Infantry	NY	Co. A
Martin, Mili	34th	Infantry	NJ	Co. G
Martin, Oscar	1st	Cavalry	LA	Co. K
Martin, Prince	5th	Infantry	MN	Co. I
Mashack, Frederick	176th	Infantry	NY	Co. F

Name	Regiment	Branch	State	Company
Mason, Charles	173rd	Cavalry	MI	Co. B
Mason, John	114th	Infantry	NY	Co. C
Mason, Joseph	106th	Infantry	OH	Co. C
Mason, Newman	106th	Infantry	OH	Co. D
Mason, Peter	118th Infantry transferred to 48th	Infantry	IL	Co. F
Mason, Wesley	13th	Infantry	ME	Co. A, E
Mason, Wesley	30th	Infantry	ME	Co. B
Matthew, Thomas	51st	Infantry	NY	Co. B
Maxwell, Daniel	3rd	Cavalry	OH	Co. K
Mayfield, John	11th	Cavalry	PA	Co. A
McAlpine, Caesar	124th	Infantry	IL	Co. A
McBee, Andrew	2nd	Lt. Arty.	MO	
McCarl, Jack	30th	Infantry	MO	Co. G
McClellan, Henry	57th	Infantry	IL	Co. E
McCord, Benjamin	65th	Infantry	IL	Co. G
McCoy, John	165th	Infantry	NY	Co B
McCoy, William	11th	Cavalry	MO	Co. G
McCracken, William	2nd	Cavalry	AK	Co. K
McCullough, William	60th	Infantry	IL	Co. D
McDade, James	4th	Cavalry	WI	Co. F
McDonald, Alfred	7th	Cavalry	PA	Co. M
McDonald, Horace	13th	Infantry	ME	Co. I
McElhannon, Thomas	4th	Cavalry	AK	Co. B
McGrew, Joseph	124th	Infantry	IL	Co. E
McGrew, Parker	32nd	Infantry	OH	Co. K
McKeal, Clayborn	72nd	Infantry	IL	Co. F
McKee, Willson	3rd Mtd.	Infantry	NC	Co. E
McKinney (McKenna), Amos	1st	Cavalry	AL	Co. C teamster
McKnight, Ellis	8th	Infantry	ME	Co. E
McLauren, Anderson	50th	Infantry	IL	Co. E
McLean, Arthur	1st	Infantry	KS	Co. B, G
McLean, Henry	7th	Heavy Art'y	NY	Co. F
McLean, Thomas	124th	Infantry	IL	Co. D
McLelian, Nash	34th	Infantry	IL	
McMichael, Isham	32nd	Infantry	NY	Co. H
McMillen, Daniel		Lt. Art'y.	NY	10th Ind. Batt'y
McMurray, James	9th	Infantry	WV	Co. C
Mead, Aleck	4th	Cavalry	IL	Co. E
Mead, William	18th	Cavalry	NY	Co. I
Meadows, Luke	98th	Infantry	NY	Co. A, B
Medley, Richard	2nd	Infantry	NH	Co. C
Medley, Richard	12th	Infantry	NH	Co. D
Meigs, Thomas	13th	Infantry	ME	Co. A
Melelian, Nash	78th	Infantry	IN	Co. G

Mercer, Raymond	58th	Infantry	PA	Co. A
Meshack, Thomas	118th	Infantry	IL	Co. A
Metcalf, Oscar	118th	Infantry	IL	Co. G
Mikes, Charles	8th	Infantry	ME	Co. C
Milam, Joseph	10th	Infantry	MO	Co. H
Miles, Cannon	34th	Infantry	IN	
Miles, Cannon	78th	Infantry	IN	Co. G
Miles, Elijah	91st	Infantry	IL	Co. K
Miles, Isaac	1st	Infantry	KS	Co. H, B
Miles, Joseph	182nd	Infantry	NY	Co. G
Miller, Charles	91st	Infantry	NY	Co. C
Miller, Edward	159th	Infantry	NY	Co. E
Miller, Elijah	72nd	Infantry	IN	Co. A
Miller, George	13th	Infantry	ME	Co. C
Miller, John D.	118th	Infantry	IL	Co. G
Miller, Peter	3rd	Cavalry	NJ	Co. E
Miller, Turner	44th	Infantry	IN	Co. E
Miller, Wesley	118th	Infantry	IL`	Co. C
Milor, Vesia	21st	Infantry	MO	Co. E
Milton, Assa	72nd	Infantry	IL	Co. F
Miner, Charles	1st	Cavalry	LA	Co. D
Mines, Benjamin	6th	Infantry	MO	Co. B
Minor, William	72nd	Infantry	IL	Co. F
Mitchel, David	9th	Infantry	ME	Co. A
Mitchell, Berry (Bery)	3rd Mtd.	Infantry	NC	Co. B
Mitchell, Fryday	1st	Infantry	KS	Co. F
Mitchell, Lewis	30th	Infantry	IL	Co. H
Mitchell, Steve	58th	Infantry	IL	Co. B
Monroe, Madison	95th	Infantry	IL	Co. A
Monroe, Madison	95th	Infantry	IN	Co. A
Moon, David	13th	Cavalry	IN	Co. I
Moore, Anderson	69th	Infantry	NY	Co. E
Moore, Anderson	121st	Infantry	NY	Co. I
Moore, Frank	4th	Cavalry	WI	Co. E
Moore, Hamilton	7th	Cavalry	PA	Co. K
Moore, Samuel	23rd	Infantry	MO	Co. D
Moore, Taylor	3rd Mtd.	Infantry	NC	Co. A
Moore, William	13th	Infantry	MI	Co. K
Moore, William	14th	Cavalry	KS	Co. D
Moran, William	12th	Infantry	IL	Co. B
Morgan, Isaac	182nd	Infantry	NY	Co. A
Morgan, William	161st	Infantry	NY	Co. B
Morrell, Paul	165th	Infantry	NY	Co. D
Morrison, David	50th	Infantry	IL	Co. F
Morrow, Alfred	32nd	Infantry	NY	Co. D

Morse, Maurice	72nd	Infantry	IL	Co. A
Moseby, John	3rd	Infantry	MN	Co. K
Moses, Dowell	117th	Infantry	IL	Co. F
Muck, James	4th	Cavalry	WI	Co. L
Mullin, William	77th	Infantry	IL	Co. G
Mullin, William	103rd	Infantry	IL	Co. B
Mumford, Henry	83rd	Infantry	IL	Co. K
Murphy, Jones	10th	Infantry	TN	Co. H
Murry, Caleb	1st	Infantry	KS	Co. F
Myers, David	162nd	Infantry	NY	Co. I
Myott, John	101st	Infantry	PA	Co. I
Nazree, Thomas	155th	Infantry	NY	Co. B
Nelson, John	57th	Infantry	IL	Co. A
Neuson, James	155th	Infantry	NY	Co. E
Newman, James	1st	Infantry	KS	Co. E
Nickerson, Alexander	90th	Infantry	NY	Co. K
Nixon, James	34th	Infantry	NJ	Co. B
Nixon, Wilson	155th	Infantry	NY	Co. C
Noah, Alexander	34th	Infantry	IL	Co. A
Noble, Edward	83rd	Infantry	IL	Co. F
Nowles, Lewis	124th	Infantry	IL	Co. B
Oakes, Stephen	7th	Cavalry	IL	Co. L
Oakley, Peter	15th	Cavalry	PA	Co. I
Oaks, Green	11th	Cavalry	MO	Co. C, M
Oliver, Hamilton	1st	Infantry	KS	Co. D
Oliver, Jeremiah	1st	Infantry	NJ	Co. K
Oliver, jerimiah	Vet. Infantry 1st	Batt'n	NJ	Co. B
Olmstead, Manuel	160th	Infantry	NY	Co. F
Olmsted, Arthur	12th	Infantry	IL	Co. I
Olmsted, Dudley	12th	Infantry	IL	Co. I
Opelesley, Augustus	Cavalry	1st Bn.	NV	Co. B
Osborn, Thomas	118th	Infantry	IL	Co. B
Ousley, John	124th	Infantry	IL	Co. G
Owens, Jesse	124th	Infantry	IL	Co. G
Owens, Stephen	129th	Infantry	IL	Co. F
Pacien (Patience), Crowder	103rd	Infantry	PA	Co. C
Page, George W.	148th	Infantry	NY	Co. E
Palmer, Benjamin	31st	Infantry	NY	Co. G
Palmer, George	113th	Infantry	NY	Co. A
Palmer, James	31st	Infantry	NY	Co. G
Palmer, James	89th	Infantry	NY	Co. K
Palmer, Moses	31st	Infantry	NY	Co. I
Palmer, Moses	89th	Infantry	NY	Co. K
Palmer, Rufus	31st	Infantry	NY	Co. F
Pancha, John	3rd	Cavalry	MI	Co. F

Name	Regiment	Branch	State	Company
Parham, John	6th	Infantry	MO	Co. B
Parker, Anderson	21st	Infantry	MO	Co. I
Parker, Cornelius	4th	Cavalry	IL	Co. A
Parker, Jones	31st	Infantry	NY	Co. I
Parker, Moses	103rd	Infantry	IL	Co. B
Parmil, William	81st	Infantry	IL	Co. C
Parrish, Caleb	4th	Cavalry	MI	Co. I
Patton, David	7th	Cavalry	PA	Co. E
Paulk, Robert	7th	Infantry	IL	Co. B
Payton, ?	19th	Infantry	MI	Co. B
Pearce, Frank	60th	Infantry	IL	Co. A
Pebles, George	1st	Infantry	KS	Co. D
Peck, Major	57th	Infantry	IL	Co. E
Pennybaker, James	102nd	Infantry	IL	Co. I
Perkins, Albert	Lt. Art'y.		NY	6th Ind. Batt'y
Perkins, Tillman	105th	Infantry	IL	Co. B
Perry, Commodore	4th	Cavalry	WI	Co. G
Perry, Edmund	91st	Infantry	NY	Co. C
Pete, Thomas	28th	Infantry	PA	Co. B
Petre, Alford C.	10th	Infantry	MO	Co. B
Phillips, Berry	34th	Infantry	IL	
Phillips, Lewis	3rd	Cavalry	MA	Co. M
Phillips, Spencer	91st	Infantry	NY	Co. H
Pickett, Nicholas	10th	Cavalry	MO	Co. E
Pierce, Frank	19th	Infantry	IL	Co. C
Pierce, John	18th	Cavalry	NY	Co. D
Pierson, Henry	10th	Infantry	MO	Co. K
Pigg, Benjamin	15th	Cavalry	PA	Co. C
Piper, Hillyard	124th	Infantry	IL	Co. A
Poe, John	2nd St. Mil.	Cavalry	MO	Co. K
Pointer, David	113th	Infantry	NY	Co. H
Pointer, Pompey	113th	Infantry	NY	Co. H
Polk, Charles E.	2nd	Infantry	CA	Co. B
Polk, Peter	105th	Infantry	IL	Co. H
Polk, Richard	8th	Infantry	CA	Co. B
Pollack, Charles	8th	Infantry	CA	Co. K
Pollard, Frank	11th	Infantry	IL	Co. E
Pollhill, William	92nd	Infantry	NY	Co. C
Pompon, Alexander	118th	Infantry	IL	Co. C
Pool (Poole), Joel	1st	Cavalry	AL	Co. E
Pool, Thomas	1st	Cavalry	AL	Co. M
Porter, James	11th	Cavalry	KS	Co. K
Porter, Thomas O.	26th	Infantry	MO	Co. H
Posey, Jubilee	31st	Infantry	IL	Co. K
Potilla, Henderson	11th	Cavalry	MO	Co. C

Name	Regiment	Branch	State	Company	
Potilla, Henderson	3rd	Cavalry	MO	Co. C, B	
Potter, Allic	30th	Infantry	MA	Co. K	
Potts, Elbert	10th	Infantry	TN	Co. G	
Powell, Alexander	48th	Infantry	IL	Co. A, F	
Powell, Allen	81st	Infantry	IL	Co. F	
Powell, George	West Eng. Reg. Vol.		MO		
Powell, George	1st	Eng.	MO	Co. D, C.	
Powell, Nathan	14th	Cavalry	KS	Co. D	
Powers, Alfred	32nd	Infantry	NY	Co. F	
Powers, Dick	3rd	Cavalry	MA	Co. F	
Pratt, Arnold	118th	Infantry	IL	Co. D	
Preston, Jackson	98th	Infantry	IL	Co. H	
Prewett (Pruit), Thomas	59th	Infantry	IL		
Price, Edwin	8th	Infantry	ME	Co. B	
Price, Jackson	3rd Mounted	Infantry	TN	Co. B	
Price, Orris	129th	Infantry	IL	Co. H	
Price, William	6th	Infantry	MO	Co. C	
Pride, Jerry	3rd	Cavalry	MI	Co. C	
Prior, Middleton	57th	Infantry	IL	Co. I	
Providence, Peter	95th	Infantry	IL	Co. K	
Prue, William	173rd	Infantry	NY	Co. A	
Pruitt, Thomas	59th	Infantry	IL	Co. D	
Pugh, Henry	85th	Infantry	NY	Co. C	
Purchase, Hector	8th	Infantry	ME	Co. B	
Putnam, Edward	2nd	Cavalry	IL	Co. K, B	
Rainer, Mark (Mack)	32nd	Infantry	NY	Co. B	
Rainy, William	21st	Infantry	MO	Co. D	
Rally, Alfred	1st	Infantry	MO	Co. I	
Ralston, Ephraim	102nd	Infantry	IL	Co. K	
Ramer, Peter	12th	Infantry	IL	Co. F	
Ramsbury, Robert E.	124th	Infantry	IL	Co. E	
Ramsey, Abraham	35th	Infantry	IL	Co. F	
Ramsey, Douglas	1st	Infantry	KS	Co. A	
Randall, William	118th	Infantry	IL	Co. B	
Rann, Jesse	116th	Infantry	NY	Co. C	
Ransom, Adam	7th	Infantry	MO	Co. I	
Ray, Samuel	11th	Cavalry	NY	Co. I	
Read (Porter), John	1st	Cavalry	AL		
Rector, Andrew	2nd	Cavalry	AK	Co. B	
Rector, Willis	2nd	Cavalry	AK	Co. B	
Redding, John F.	3rd	Cavalry	NJ	Co. G	
Reed, George	West Eng. Reg. Vol.		MO	Co. C	*
Reedus, Morgan	12th	Infantry	IL	Co. K	
Reese, Zenon	118th	Infantry	IL	Co. C	
Reynolds, Richard	48th	Infantry	IL	Co. D	

Name	Unit	Branch	State	Company
Reynolds, Ashley	99th	Infantry	NY	Co. B, C
Reynolds, Ashley	137th	Infantry	NY	Co. H
Reynolds, Jasper	10th	Infantry	IL	Co. C
Reynolds, Shadrack	7th	Infantry	IL	Co. K
Rice, David	7th	Cavalry	PA	Co. A
Rice, Frank	31st	Infantry	MA	Co. G
Rice, William	3rd	Cavalry	NJ	Co. B
Richards, John	3rd	Cavalry	MI	Co. H
Richardson, Dick	16th	Cavalry	KS	Co. G
Richardson, Dick	1st	Infantry	KS	Co. G
Richie, Thomas	8th	Infantry	CA	Co. D
Riggins, Horatio	1st	Infantry	MO	Co. F
Riley, Stephen	8th	Infantry	ME	Co. B
Ripley, Joseph	1st	Infantry	KS	Co. G
Ritterson, Sam	98th	Infantry	NY	Co. B
Rivers, Emery	1st	Cavalry	AL	Co. E teamster
Roberson, Andrew	1st	Infantry	KS	Co. D
Roberts, Isaac	1st	Cavalry	AL	Co. M teamster
Roberts, Isaac	117th	Infantry	IL	Co. A
Roberts, William	62nd	Infantry	IL	Co. G
Robertson, Anthony	1st	Infantry	NJ	Co. K
Robinson, Cornelius	1st Lt. Arty. Batt'y		PA	Co. E
Robinson, Henry	2nd	Infantry	MD	Co. G
Robinson, John	8th	Infantry	CT	Co. H
Robinson, Joseph R.	Cavalry 1st Bn.		NV	Co. B
Robinson, Joseph	1st Lt. Art'y		MI	Batt'y E
Robinson, Peter	13th	Infantry	ME	Co. F
Robison, Philip	55th	Infantry	PA	Co. H
Robison, Toby	55th	Infantry	PA	Co. H
Roche, David	1st	Infantry	LA	Co. C
Rodgers, Green	22nd	Infantry	IN	Co. D
Rodgers, Green	82nd	Infantry	IN	Co. D
Rodgers, Sidney	32nd	Infantry	NY	Co. K
Rodgers, William	48th	Infantry	IL	Co. D
Roe, John	2nd	Infantry	CT	Co. G
Rogan, James	102nd	Infantry	IL	Co. G
Rogers, Henry	182nd	Infantry	NY	Co. K
Rohaman, George	2nd	Cavalry	CA	Co. H
Rolac/Roulhac, John	85th	Infantry	NY	Co. C
Rone, Daniel	93rd	Infantry	IL	Co. G
Rooker, Handy	15th	Cavalry	PA	Co. C
Rooks, Joseph (James)	7th	Cavalry	MO	Co. M
Ross, Albert	72nd	Infantry	IL	Co. H

Name	Unit	Branch	State	Company
Ross, Robert	11th	Infantry	MO	Co. G
Roundtree, Martin		Lt. Art'y.	NY	11th Ind. Batt'y
Roundtree, Martin		Lt. Art'y.	NY	5th Ind. Batt'y
Rowler, Henry	162nd	Infantry	NY	Co. B
Rowler, Henry	174th	Infantry	NY	Co. B
Rubin, Roder	7th	Infantry	MO	Co. G
Runnel, Spencer	57th	Infantry	IL	Co. E
Runnells, Thomas	21st	Infantry	MO	Co. E
Russell, George W.	32nd	Infantry	NY	Co. A
Russell, Henry	102nd	Infantry	IL	Co. E
Russell, William	51st	Infantry	NY	Co. H
Ruth, Isaac	8th	St. Mil. Cav.	MO	Co. L
Rutledge, John	6th	Infantry	CA	Co. B
Ryan, Thomas	35th	Infantry	MO	Co. E
Sachell, W.	96th	Infantry	NY	Co. A
Samuel, Sampson	59th	Infantry	IL	Co. F
Sanders, Ben	55th	Infantry	PA	Co. K
Sanders, Calein (Calvin)	1st	Infantry	KS	Co. E
Sanders, S????	1st	Lt. Art'y. Btt'y.	MO	Co. K
Sanders, Simon		Lt. Art'y	KS	2nd Ind. Btt'y
Sanders, Simon		Lt. Art'y.	KS	3rd Ind. Btt'y.
Sands, Robert H.	38th	Infantry	MA	Co. B
Saunders, George	23rd	Infantry	MO	Co. K
Saunders, Ned	3rd	Infantry	MN	Co. B
Savage, James	164th	Infantry	MO	Co. G
Schadrick, Bill	58th	Infantry	IL	Co. A
Scippio	8th	Infantry	ME	Co. D
Scott, Benjamin	32nd	Infantry	NY	Co. F
Scott, Burrill	31st	Infantry	MA	Co. G, C
Scott, George	3rd	Cavalry	MI	
Scott, Harry	8th	Infantry	ME	Co. E
Scott, Nathan	162nd	Infantry	NY	Co. C
Scott, Thomas	2nd	Cavalry	IL	Co. H, E
Scott, William	3rd	Cavalry	NJ	Co. K
Scott, William	118th	Infantry	IL	Co. G
Scudder, Aaron	34th	Infantry	NJ	Co. E
Seabrook, Ansel	4th	Cavalry	MA	Co. L
Seabrook, Ansel	1st	Cavalry	MA	Co. L
Semmes, Joseph	3rd	Cavalry	MA	Co. D
Seymore, Antoine	4th	Cavalry	WI	Co. I
Shades, Albert	124th	Infantry	IL	Co. A
Shanon (Sharon, Shawn), Owen	1st	Cavalry	AL	Co. G teamster
Sharp, Robert	1st	Infantry	KS	Co. E
Sharp, William Henry		Infantry 1st Bn.	NV	Co. A

Name	Regiment	Branch	State	Company
Shaw, Henry	11th	Cavalry	IL	Co. K
Shelby, Maddison	31st	Infantry	MA	Co. E
Shellant, Ensley	7th	Infantry	MO	Co. H
Shepard, Nelson	Lt. Art'y		NY	24th Ind. Btt'y
Sheppard, Edward	1st New Orleans Inf.		LA	Co. E
Sheppard, Edward	1st	Infantry	LA	Co. F
Sheppard, Jeremiah	99th	Infantry	NY	Co. B
Sheppard, Jerimiah	132nd	Infantry	NY	Co. C
Sheridan, Henry S.	124th	Infantry	IL	Co. D
Sherod, Bob	3rd	Cavalry	MI	Co. M
Shields, James	6th Hvy. Art'y		MI	Co. G
Shook, Edward	8th	Infantry	KS	Co. A
Shook, Isaac	8th	Infantry	KS	Co. A
Showell, Shadriac	9th	Infantry	MI	Co. C
Sidney, Washington	160th	Infantry	NY	Co. I
Silor, Joseph	1st	Cavalry	MO	Co. M
Simes, Elijah	6th	Cavalry	MO	Co. H
Simes, Martin	121st	Infantry	NY	Co. K
Simes, Martin	69th	Infantry	NY	Co. K
Simmons, Hosea	45th	Infantry	IL	Co. K
Simmons, William E.	13th	Infantry	ME	Co. I
Simms, Henry	160th	Infantry	NY	Co. C
Simms, James	124th	Infantry	IL	Co. E
Simons, Moses	45th	Infantry	IL	Co. G
Simons, Peter	7th	Infantry	CT	Co. K
Simpson, Amos	11th	Cavalry	MO	Co. F
Simpson, Frederick	10th	Infantry	MO	Co. F
Simpson, Jefferson	7th	Infantry	IL	Co. K
Simpson, Julius	11th	Cavalry	MO	Co. F
Simson, James	173rd	Infantry	NY	Co. D
Singleton, William	1st	Cavalry	AL	Co. C
Sisson, Silas	1st	Infantry	KS	Co. E
Skater, E.	155th	Infantry	NY	Co. D
Skoggs, Frank	48th	Infantry	IL	Co. B
Sloan, Ira	11th	Cavalry	MO	Co. B
Small, Napoleon/Nabuka	55th	Infantry	PA	Co. C
Small, Stephen	1st	Cavalry	MA	Co. K
Smart, John	160th	Infantry	NY	Co. K
Smith, Alfred	1st	Cavalry	NE	Co. K
Smith, Bailey	10th	Infantry	MO	Co. G
Smith, Claiborne	1st	Cavalry	LA	Co. B
Smith, Dandy	1st	Infantry	KS	Co. I
Smith, Francis	2nd Lt. Arty. Btty.		MO	Co. C
Smith, Frederick	160th	Infantry	NY	Co. D
Smith, Henderson	5th	Cavalry	TN	Co. B

Smith, Hiram	12th	Infantry	IL	Co. B
Smith, Horace	1st	Infantry	KS	Co. G
Smith, Isaac	4th	Cavalry	WI	Co. C
Smith, Jack	8th	Infantry	MO	Co. B
Smith, Jacob	10th	Cavalry	MI	Co. F
Smith, James R.	72nd	Infantry	IL	Co. B
Smith, James	1st	Infantry	CA	Co. B
Smith, James	1st	Infantry	LA	Co. K
Smith, Jesse	118th	Infantry	IL	Co. E
Smith, Jonas	58th	Infantry	PA	Co. D
Smith, Joseph	55th	Infantry	PA	Co. B
Smith, Joseph	8th	Infantry	ME	Co. B
Smith, Leander	13th	Infantry	ME	Co. E, A
Smith, Levi	48th	Infantry	IL	Co. F
Smith, Nelson	44th	Infantry	IN	Co. D
Smith, Nelson	72nd	Infantry	IN	Co. G
Smith, Orin	8th	Infantry	NH	Co. A
Smith, Philip	7th	Cavalry	PA	Co. F
Smith, Pompey	6th	Infantry	MO	Co. G
Smith, Rolla D.	50th	Infantry	IL	Co. A
Smith, Samuel	3rd	Cavalry	MO	Co. A
Smith, Samuel	50th	Infantry	IL	Co. G
Smith, Samuel	11th	Cavalry	MO	Co. A
Smith, Thomas	4th	Cavalry	WI	Co. I
Smith, Tony	6th	Cavalry	IL	Co. M
Smith, William	32nd	Infantry	NY	Co. E
Smith, William	8th	Infantry	VT	Co. H
Smith, Wilson	18th	Infantry	MO	Co. C
Sneed, Ezekiah	12th	Infantry	IL	Co. K
Snipe, Abraham	55th	Infantry	PA	Co. C
Snipe, Ishmael	55th	Infantry	PA	Co. C
Snoddy, Jerimiah	5th	Cavalry	KS	Co. L
Snowden, Lewis	51st	Infantry	NY	Co. C
Snowden, Lewis	109th	Infantry	NY	Co. C
Speer, Albert G.	7th	Cavalry	KS	Co. A
Spencer, John	8th	Infantry	ME	Co. H
Spencer, Richard	Lt. Art'y		AK	1st Batt'y
Spencer, Samuel	2nd	Cavalry	IL	Co. I
Spencer, Samuel	Lt. Art'y		AK	1st Batt'y
Spencer, Thomas	Lt. Art'y		AK	1st Batt'y
Spencer, Washington	Lt. Art'y		AK	1st Batt'y
Spite, James	21st	Infantry	MO	Co. B
Spohn, Ruby	162nd	Infantry	NY	Co. C
Squash, John	1st New Orleans Inf.		LA	Co. A
Squash, John	1st	Infantry	LA	Co. E

Name	Regiment	Branch	State	Company
Stadon, Randall	1st	Infantry	NC	Co. I
Stanley, Rufus	1st	Infantry	KS	Co. A
Stapleton, Steiger	83rd	Infantry	IL	Co. F
Steel, Green	48th	Infantry	IL	Co. B
Stelman, Peooher	12th	Infantry	ME	
Stephens, George E.	26th	Infantry	PA	
Stephenson, Jackson	113th	Infantry	CT	Co. F
Stephenson, Joseph	2nd	Infantry	NH	Co. G
Stephenson, Joseph	12th	Infantry	NH	Co. A
Sterns, Frank	13th	Infantry	ME	Co. B
Stevens, Alexander	78th	Infantry	IL	Co. A
Stewart, Alexander	50th	Infantry	IL	Co. E
Stewart, John	13th	Infantry	ME	Co. E
Stewart, Stephen	7th	Cavalry	PA	Co. K
Stewart, William	8th	Infantry	VT	Co. I
Still, Andrew Jackson	9th	Infantry	WV	Co. C
Still, David				
Still, David	63rd	Infantry	NY	Co. C
Still, George Washington	13th	Infantry	WV	Co. I
Still, Henry	9th	Infantry	WV	Co. F
Stokes, Robert	6th	Infantry	MO	Co. F
Stone, Jacob	19th	Infantry	MI	Co. F
Strange, Isaac	4th	Cavalry	WI	Co. E
Stratton, Stewart	50th	Infantry	IL	Co. I
Strothers, Joshua	32nd	Infantry	NY	Co. E
Stubbs, Alexander	10th	Infantry	MO	Co. G
Suggs, Edward	58th	Infantry	PA	Co. B
Suggs, Henry	58th	Infantry	PA	Co. B
Sullivan, George	3rd Lt. Art'y.	Battery	NY	Co. C
Sullivan, Israel	62nd	Infantry	IL	Co. F
Sweet, Prince	3rd	Cavalry	MI	Co. I
Swinney, Jorden	6th	Cavalry	IL	Co. M
Talbot, Ike	13th	Cavalry	IL	Co. A, K
Tasco, William J.	Infantry	1st Bn.	NV	Co. C
Tate, Lawrence	6th	Infantry	MO	Co. D
Taylor, Abner	18th	Infantry	IL	Co. I
Taylor, Benjamin	4th	Cavalry	IL	Co. B
Taylor, Britton	8th	Infantry	IL	Co. B
Taylor, Britton	17th	Infantry	IL	Co. G
Taylor, Elijah	30th	Infantry	IL	Co. C
Taylor, Gabriel	8th	Infantry	MO	Co. K
Taylor, Henry C.	18th	Infantry	IL	Co. B
Taylor, Isham	26th	Infantry	MO	Co. K
Taylor, Isham	24th	Infantry	MO	Co. E
Taylor, James	1st	Infantry	NC	Co. E

Name	Regiment	Branch	State	Company
Taylor, Jim	9th	Infantry	IL	Co. C, F
Taylor, John T.	8th	Cavalry	MO	Co. A
Taylor, Reuben	124th	Infantry	IL	Co. E
Taylor, Rice	10th	Infantry	IL	Co. C
Taylor, Richard	21st	Infantry	MO	Co. A
Taylor, Thomas	7th	St. Mil. Cavalry	MO	Co. F
Taylor, Wylie	118th	Infantry	IL	Co. H
Tedwell, John	18th Infantry transferred to 48th	Infantry	IL	Co. G
Tedwell, Thornton	18th Infantry transferred to 48th	Infantry	IL	Co. G
Teel, Ashleigh	5th	Heavy Art'y	RI	
Teel, Edmund	5th	Heavy Art'y	RI	Co. E
Tefler, James	62nd	Infantry	IL	Co. G
Telles, James	19th	Infantry	MI	Co. G
Telles, Jonathan	19th	Infantry	MI	Co. G
Temple, William	62nd	Infantry	IL	Co. G
Tennessee, John	62nd	Infantry	IL	Co. A
Terry, Garland	1st	Cavalry	AL	Co. E teamster
Thadeus, Francis	10th	Infantry	MO	Co. H
Thiesan, George	6th	Infantry	MO	Co. A
Thomas, Alexander	26th	Infantry	MO	Co. A
Thomas, Edmund	4th	Cavalry	WI	Co. I
Thomas, George	51st	Infantry	NY	Co. C
Thomas, George	160th	Infantry	NY	Co. A
Thomas, George	164th	Infantry	NY	Co. E
Thomas, John	19th	Cavalry	PA	Co. A
Thomas, John	4th	Cavalry	WI	Co. C
Thomas, John	55th	Infantry	IL	Co. D
Thomas, Nathaniel	32nd	Infantry	NY	Co. F
Thomas, Tom Henry	133rd	Infantry	NY	Co. I
Thomas, William	19th	Infantry	MI	Co. D
Thompson, Francis	3rd	Cavalry	NJ	Co. I
Thompson, George	165th	Infantry	NY	Co. D
Thompson, John	24th	Infantry	MA	
Thompson, John	98th	Infantry	NY	Co. D
Thompson, Moses	4th	Cavalry	WI	Co. F
Thompson, Peter	3rd	Cavalry	MA	Co. M
Thompson, Preston	3rd	Infantry	CO	Hospital Cook
Thompson, William	118th	Infantry	IL	Co. K
Thomson, Richard	4th	Infantry	MN	Co. H
Thornson, Jackson	66th	Infantry	IL	Co. D
Thornton, Luke	30th	Infantry	MO	Co. C
Tibbs, Elias	124th	Infantry	IL	Co. E
Tichnor, Jacob	2nd	Cavalry	MO	
Tille, Augustus	3rd	U.S. Res. Corp Infantry	MO	

Tinley, Michael	87th	Infantry	IL	Co. F
Titsworth, Willis	24th	Infantry	MO	Co. I, H
Tittsworth, Willis	21st	Infantry	MO	Co. C
Todd, John	1st	Infantry	KS	Co. H
Toliver, George	8th	Infantry	IL	Co. E
Toliver, Ned	98th	Infantry	IL	Co. B
Torian, Archy	42nd	Infantry	IL	Co. K
Torpin, Isaac	15th	Infantry	ME	Co. E
Tost, Henry	1st	Cavalry	LA	
Tow, Israel	164th	Infantry	NY	Co. C
Townson, Randal	7th	Cavalry	PA	Co. E
Trempleau, Joseph	4th	Cavalry	WI	Co. H
Trempleau, Thomas	4th	Cavalry	WI	Co. H
Tucker, Augustus	15th	Infantry	MO	Co. K
Tucker, Charles	34th	Infantry	NJ	Co. E, G
Tucker, George	118th Infantry transferred to 48th	Infantry	IL	Co. G
Tucker, Samuel	8th	Infantry	MO	Co. H
Tucker, William	130th	Infantry	IL	Co. C
Turk, Josiah	92nd	Infantry	NY	Co. F
Turner, Anthony	7th	Cavalry	IL	Co. F
Turner, Hanibal	12th	Infantry	IL	Co. G
Turner, James	99th	Infantry	NY	Co. B
Turner, James	132nd	Infantry	NY	Co. I
Turner, Leroy	30th	Infantry	IL	Co. A
Turner, Stephen	91st	Infantry	NY	Co. B
Turner, Thomas	8th	Infantry	IN	Co. C
Turner, Washington	162nd	Infantry	NY	Co. E
Twitchell, Felix	11th	Cavalry	MO	Co. H
Tyre, Ned	13th	Infantry	ME	Co. H
Udley, Lee	18th	Infantry	IL	Co. A
Van Donelson	43rd	Infantry	IL	Co. C
Vaughn, Gabriel	16th	Cavalry	KS	Co. G
Vaughn, Gabriel	1st	Infantry	KS	Co. K
Vaughn, Thomas	32nd	Infantry	NY	Co. E
Vickers, James	118th	Infantry	IL	Co. I
Vickers, Peter J.	8th	Infantry	CA	Co. K
Vigle, William	3rd	Cavalry	PA	Co. G
Viley, Charles	1st	Infantry	KS	Co. F
Vincent, George	3rd	Cavalry	MI	Co. H
Waddlow, Nelson	2nd	Lt. Art'y.	MO	Btt'y. I
Wade, Charley	81st	Infantry	IL	Co. G
Wade, David	1st	Infantry	KS	Co. K
Wadley, Samuel	32nd	Infantry	NY	Co. G
Wagdon,, John	21st	Infantry	MO	Co. A
Walker, George	18th	Cavalry	NY	Co. C

Walker, George	43rd	Infantry	IL	Co. A
Walker, Green	133rd	Infantry	NY	Co. K
Walker, Henry	4th	Cavalry	WI	Co. B
Walker, Isaac	3rd	Cavalry	NY	Co. F
Walker, James	132nd	Infantry	NY	Co. A
Walker, John	102nd	Infantry	IL	Co. C
Walker, Squire	2nd	Lt. Art'y.	MO	Btt'y. K
Walker, William	22nd	Cavalry	NY	Co. I
Wallace, Charles	173rd	Infantry	NY	Co. F
Wallace, John	3rd	Cavalry	NJ	Co. K
Wallace, Toby M.	118th	Infantry	IL	Co. C
Walton, (Waldron, Waller, Walter), Stephen	1st	Cavalry	AL	Co. C
Walton, William	129th	Infantry	IL	Co. B
Ward, Jerry	1st	Infantry	NC	Co. B
Warner, John	12th	Infantry	IL	Co. E
Warner, Preston	89th	Infantry	IL	Co. H
Warren, Cornelius	12th	Infantry	IL	Co. A
Warren, King	10th	Infantry	MO	Co. A
Warren, King	26th	Infantry	MO	Co. K
Warren, Major	12th	Infantry (transf. to USCT) teamster		
Warren, Patrick	12th	Infantry	IL	Co. C
Warwick, David	1st	Infantry	LA	Co. I
Washington, Aaron	57th	Infantry	IL	Co. D
Washington, Benjamin	19th	Infantry	MI	Co. D
Washington, Dougherty	8th	Infantry	MO	Co. E
Washington, George	3rd	Lt. Arty.	NY	Co. L
Washington, George	4th	Cavalry	IL	Co. E
Washington, George	10th	Infantry	IL	Co. G
Washington, George	28th	Infantry	KY	Co. C
Washington, George	53rd	Infantry	IL	Co. C
Washington, George	55th	Infantry	IL	Co. K
Washington, George	66th	Infantry	IL	Co. D
Washington, George	6th	Infantry	MO	Co. F
Washington, George	72nd	Infantry	IL	Co. I
Washington, George	81st	Infantry	IL	Co. D
Washington, George	8th	Infantry	MO	Co. I
Washington, George	91st	Infantry	NY	Co. E
Washington, George	15th	Infantry	IN	Co. C
Washington, George	25th	Infantry	IN	Co. D
Washington, George	26th	Infantry	IN	Co. F
Washington, George	46th	Infantry	IN	Co. H
Washington, George	9th	Infantry	MI	Co. E
Washington, George	118th	Infantry	IL	Co. C
Washington, George	124th	Infantry	IL	Co. B
Washington, George	159th	Infantry	NY	Co. B

Washington, George	162nd	Infantry	NY	Co. I
Washington, George	21st	Infantry	MO	Co. B
Washington, George	8th	Infantry	KS	Co. A
Washington, Henry	1st	Cavalry	LA	Co. G
Washington, Joseph	165th	Infantry	NY	Co. B
Washington, Thomas	6th	Infantry	MO	Co. B
Watkins, Albert G.	22nd	Infantry	IL	Co B
Watkins, Bell	18th	Infantry	MO	Co. B
Watkins, Henry	95th	Infantry	IL	Co. A
Watkins, Primus	3rd	Cavalry	MO	Co. K
Watson, Allen W.	2nd	Cavalry	MN	Co. G
Watson, Frederick	4th	Cavalry	WI	Co. E
Watson, Madison	32nd	Infantry	NY	Co. G
Watson, Manuel	62nd	Infantry	IL	Co. F
Watson, Robert	34th	Infantry	IL	
Watson, Robert	34th	Infantry	IN	
Watson, Robert	78th	Infantry	IN	Co. I
Weatherly, Alfred	46th	Infantry	IL	Co. B
Weaver, Tom	3rd	Cavalry	MI	Co. M
Wells, Ephraim	13th	Infantry	CT	Co. A
Wells, James	3rd Mtd. Infantry		NC	Co. B
Wells, Moses	1st	Cavalry	LA	Co. I
Wells, Richard	45th	Infantry	IL	Co. G
Wells, William	Lt. Art'y.		MA	6th Ind. Battery
Welsley, Frederick	1st	Cavalry	LA	Co. G
Welsley, Henry	1st	Cavalry	LA	Co. B
Wesley, John	2nd St. Mil. Calvary		MO	Co. F
Wesley, John	3rd	Infantry	MN	Co. D
Wesr, Hopkins	13th	Infantry	MI	Co. K
West, James	15th	Infantry	MO	Co. C
West, Peter	66th	Infantry	IL	Co. A
West, Richard	103rd	Infantry	PA	Co. I
West, Simon (Simeon)	1st	Cavalry	AL	Co. H
Weston, John	72nd	Infantry	IL	Co. F
Wethington, Abraham	19th	Infantry	MI	Co. D
While, Thomas W.	4th	Cavalry	WI	Co. L
White, Alexander	3rd	Cavalry	NJ	Co. M
White, Charles	45th	Infantry	IL	Co. A
White, Daniel	66th	Infantry	IL	Co. G
White, Jacob	18th	Infantry	MO	Co. D
White, John L.	44th	Infantry	IN	Co. D
White, John L.	72nd	Infantry	IN	Co. D
White, Philip H.	92nd	Infantry	IL	Co. K
White, Robert	1st New Orleans Inf.		LA	Co. H
White, Robert	1st	Infantry	LA	Co. H

White, Thomas	9th	Infantry	IL	Co. C teamster
White, Thomas	50th	Infantry	IL	Co. G
White, William	1st	Hvy. Art'y.	MN	Co. A
White, Wilson	4th	Cavalry	WI	Co. D
Whitecar, Jacob	6th	Infantry	MO	Co. B
Whitehead, Henry	99th	Infantry	NY	Co. B
Whitey, Solimon	1st	Infantry	KS	Co. B
Whitfield, Henry	10th	Cavalry	MO	Co. C
Whitfield, Marshall	11th	Infantry	MO	Co. B
Whiticar, Isaac	18th	Infantry	MO	Co. E
Whitley, Edward	21st	Infantry	MO	Co. B
Wilburne, Milton	Lt. Att'y.		MN	1st Ind. Btt'y
Wilder, Gansey	30th	Infantry	MA	Co. H
Wiley, Emroy	20th	Infantry	IL	Co. A
Wilkes, Abraham	18th	Infantry	IL	Co. I
Wilkins, Henry	2nd	Cavalry	IL	Co. K, B
Williams, Albert	4th	Cavalry	WI	Co. D
Williams, Albert	132nd	Infantry	NY	Co. E
Williams, Alfred	1st	Infantry	KS	Co. F
Williams, Alonzo	1st	Infantry	KS	Co. B
Williams, Andrew J.	1st	Cavalry	AL	Co. I
Williams, Billy	8th	Infantry	MO	Co. D
Williams, George	9th	Infantry	IL	Co. E
Williams, George	32nd	Infantry	NY	Co. A
Williams, George	2nd	Cavalry	CA	Co. D
Williams, George	118th	Infantry	IL	Co. E
Williams, Gilbert	8th	Infantry	KS	Co. K
Williams, Henry	72nd	Infantry	IL	Co. K
Williams, Henry	10th	Infantry	MO	Co. H
Williams, Isaac	124th	Infantry	IL	Co. I
Williams, James	11th	Cavalry	IL	Co. C
Williams, James	1st New Orleans Inf.		LA	Co. A
Williams, James	1st	Infantry	LA	Co. A
Williams, Jeremiah	1st	Cavalry	FL	Co. C
Williams, Jesse	18th	Infantry	MO	Co. G
Williams, John	30th	Infantry	MO	Co. F
Williams, Joseph	1st	Cavalry	LA	Co. I
Williams, Joseph	21st	Infantry	MO	Co. F
Williams, King	18th	Infantry	MO	Co. I
Williams, Perry	6th	Cavalry	MO	Co. G
Williams, Peter	31st	Infantry	MA	Co. D, I
Williams, Riley	1st	Infantry	NC	Co. A
Williams, Sidney	32nd	Infantry	NY	Co. G
Williams, Thomas	2nd	Lt. Art'y.	MO	Btt'y. A

Williams, Zachariah	81st	Infantry	IL	Co. F
Williamson, Paul	30th	Infantry	ME	Co. B
Willis, Pauldo	132nd	Infantry	NY	Co. G
Wills, Ireland	11th	Cavalry	MO	Co. E
Wilson, D.	1st	Infantry	KS	Co. D
Wilson, Fonrose	10th	Infantry	IL	Co. B
Wilson, Henry	3rd	Cavalry	NJ	Co. M
Wilson, John	34th	Infantry	NJ	Co. B, K
Wilson, Peter	3rd	Cavalry	MI	Co. C
Wilson, Robert	3rd Mtd. Infantry		NC	Co. A
Wilson, Thomas	3rd	Cavalry	PA	Co. G
Wilson, Wesley	83rd	Infantry	IL	Co. K
Wilson, William	3rd	Cavalry	MI	Co. C
Winston, Samuel	21st	Infantry	MO	Co. E
Winters, Edward	13th	Cavalry	IL	Co. D
Winters, Henry	124th	Infantry	IL	Co. D
Woan, Andy	21st	Infantry	MO	Co. E
Wood, James	128th	Infantry	NY	Co K
Wood, Robert	15th	Infantry	MO	Co. I
Wood, Thomas	83rd	Infantry	IL	Co. A
Woodford, John	72nd	Infantry	IL	Co. C
Woodlow, Henry	26th	Infantry	MA	Co. E
Woods, Joseph	72nd	Infantry	IL	Co. E
Woods, Robert	2nd	Infantry	MO	Co. I
Woodson, Henry	66th	Infantry	IL	Co. A
Wooley, Edward	12th	Infantry	IL	Co. K
Abernathy, George	66th	Infantry	IN	Co. C
Wright, Henry	1st	Cavalry	CO	Co. E
Wright, James	3rd	Cavalry	NJ	Co. A, I, M
Wright, John	1st Bn.	Cavalry	NV	Co. D
Wright, William	7th	Cavalry	MO	Co. I
Yerbe, John	2nd	Infantry	NH	Co. E
Yerbe, John	12th	Infantry	NH	Co. C
York, Hugh (Huell)	23rd	Infantry	MO	Co. A
York, Nelson	23rd	Infantry	MO	Co. B
York, Thomas	23rd	Infantry	MO	Co. B
Yost, Gabriel	71st	Infantry	NY	Co. G
Young, Berry	1st	Infantry	KS	Co. I
Young, Charles	1st	Cavalry	LA	Co. I, E
Young, Jasper	89th	Infantry	NY	Co. K
Young, Moses	21st	Infantry	MO	Co. E
Young, Thomas	21st	Infantry	MO	Co. E
Young, Willis	8th	Infantry	NH	Co. A
Younger, Joseph	30th	Infantry	MA	Co. K

BLACK SOLDIERS BY STATES

☆ALABAMA

Davis, Bird	1st	Cavalry	Co. D
Davis, William	1st	Cavalry	Co. M
Farmer (Forman), Simon	1st	Cavalry	Co. A
McKinney (McKenna), Amos	1st	Cavalry	Co. C
Pool, Thomas	1st	Cavalry	teamster Co. M
Pool (Poole), Joel	1st	Cavalry	Co. E
Read (Porter), John	1st	Cavalry	
Rivers, Emery	1st	Cavalry	Co. E
Roberts, Isaac	1st	Cavalry	teamster Co. M
Shanon (Sharon, Shawn), Owen	1st	Cavalry	teamster Co. G
Singleton, William	1st	Cavalry	teamster Co. C
Terry, Garland	1st	Cavalry	Co. E
Walton, (Waldron, Waller, Walter), Stephen	1st	Cavalry	teamster Co. C
West, Simon (Simeon)	1st	Cavalry	Co. H
Williams, Andrew J.	1st	Cavalry	Co. I

☆ARKANSAS

Buchanan, Adam	Lt. Art'y		1st Batt'y
Crawford, David	Lt. Art'y		1st Batt'y
Crawford, William H.	Lt. Art'y		1st Batt'y
Draiton, Govern E.	2nd	Cavalry	Co. D
McCracken, William	2nd	Cavalry	Co. K
McElhannon, Thomas	4th	Cavalry	Co. B
Rector, Andrew	2nd	Cavalry	Co. B
Rector, Willis	2nd	Cavalry	Co. B
Spencer, Richard	Lt. Art'y		1st Batt'y
Spencer, Samuel	Lt. Art'y		1st Batt'y
Spencer, Thomas	Lt. Art'y		1st Batt'y

☆CALIFORNIA

Anderson, George	6th	Infantry	Co. B
Crawford, Richard	8th	Infantry	Co. B
Edwards, Alexander	2nd	Cavalry	Co. A
Francis, Henry C.	6th	Infantry	Co. B
Graffell, Charles	2nd	Cavalry	Co. H
Hutchinson, James	8th	Infantry	Co. B
Lajenne, John Lewis	8th	Infantry	Co. D
Lambert, William H.	2nd	Cavalry	Co. D
Polk, Charles E.	2nd	Infantry	Co. B
Polk, Richard	8th	Infantry	Co. B
Pollack, Charles	8th	Infantry	Co. K
Richie, Thomas	8th	Infantry	Co. D
Rohaman, George	2nd	Cavalry	Co. H
Rutledge, John	6th	Infantry	Co. B
Smith, James	1st	Infantry	Co. B
Vickers, Peter J.	8th	Infantry	Co. K
Williams, George	2nd	Cavalry	Co. D

☆COLORADO TERRITORY

Botts, William	3rd	Cavalry	Co. E
Bradford, Sandy	1st	Cavalry	Co. G
Brooks, Charles	1st	Cavalry	Co. G
Brown, Benjamin	1st	Cavalry	Co. H, G
Davis, James	1st	Cavalry	Co. B, F
Davis, Samuel	2nd	Cavalry	Co. K
Ellix, Thomas L.	1st	Cavalry	Co. G
Ficklin, Gabriel	1st	Cavalry	Co. B, E
Hughes, Green	2nd	Cavalry	Co. K
Thompson, Preston	3rd	Infantry	Hospital Cook
Wright, Henry	1st	Cavalry	Co. E

☆CONNECTICUT

Carter, Edward	7th	Infantry	Co. I
Clark, William	15th	Infantry	Co. D
Cook, Frederick	8th	Infantry	Co. F
Forbes, George	12th	Infantry	Co. A
Jackson, Thomas	9th	Infantry	Co. F

Johnson, Oliver	8th	Infantry	Co. I
Johnson, William Henry	2nd	Infantry	
Johnson, William H.	8th	Infantry	
Jones, Samuel	8th	Infantry	Co. A
Simons, Peter	7th	Infantry	Co. K
?Stephenson, Jackson	113th	Infantry	Co. F
Robinson, John	8th	Infantry	Co. H
?Roe, John	2nd	Infantry	Co. G
Wells, Ephraim	13th	Infantry	Co. A

☆**DAKOTA TERRITORY** None

☆**DELAWARE** None

☆**DISTRICT OF COLUMBIA** None

☆**FLORIDA**

Barker, John	1st	Cavalry	Co. D
Brannon, Moses	2nd	Cavalry	Co. C
Banks, Eli F.	1st	Cavalry	Co. C
Horton, Wiliford	1st	Cavalry	Co. C
Jones, Matthew	1st	Cavalry	Co. E
Jones, Richard	1st	Cavalry	Co. F
Locklin, Erastus M.	1st	Cavalry	Hospital
Williams, Jeremiah	1st	Cavalry	Co. C

☆**GEORGIA** None

☆**ILLINOIS**

Abbott, Benjamin	95th	Infantry	Co. H
Adams, Jackson	29th	Infantry	Co. C
Adkins, Jacob	52nd	Infantry	Co. F
Albert, Prince	54th	Infantry	Co. A
Alexander, George	62nd	Infantry	Co. F
Alexander, Noah	78th	Infantry	Co. A
Alsbrook, Joseph	25th	Infantry	Co. I
Anderson, Alexander	8th	Infantry	Co. C
Anderson, Charles H.	59th	Infantry	Co. B
Anderson, Charles	89th	Infantry	Co. B
Anderson, John	12th	Infantry	
Anderson, Lewis	28th	Infantry	Co. K
Anderson, Lewis	91st	Infantry	Co. K

Anderson, Morris	72nd	Infantry	Co. D
Andrews, Edmond	83rd	Infantry	Co. F
Anthony, Albert	4th	Cavalry	Co. I
Anthony, Jasper	4th	Cavalry	Co. B, I
Anthony, Jasper	12th	Cavalry	Co. I
Archy, Torian	42nd	Infantry	Co. K
Armstead, Albert	118th	Infantry	Co. A
Armstead, Stark	9th	Infantry	
Armstead, Willis	52nd	Infantry	Co. D
Arnold, Oliver	118th	Infantry	Co. D
Ash, Reuben	8th	Infantry	Co. C
Austin, Porter	28th	Infantry	Co. G
Austin, Porter	91st	Infantry	Co. H
Austin, Samuel	95th	Infantry	Co. F
Ayers, Peter	105th	Infantry	Co. D
Bachelor, Ned	1st	Lt. Atty.	Btty. D
Bailey, Charles	9th	Infantry	Co. C
Bailey, Richard	83rd	Infantry	Co. A
Baker, Washington	124th	Infantry	Co. H
Balentine, Henry	52nd	Infantry	Co. K
Baldwin, Charles	124th	Infantry	Co. K
Banes, Preston	1st	Lt. Arty	Btty B
Banks, Richard	14th	Cavalry	Co. I
Barber, Handy	66th	Infantry	Co. B
Bards, John E.	102nd	Infantry	Co. I
Barnes, David	98th	Infantry	Co. A
Barnes, Henry	118th	Infantry	Co. H
Barnes, Sandy	2nd	Lt. Atty.	Btty C
Barzine, Solomon	81st	Infantry	Co. D
Bass, Alfred	98th	Infantry	Co. B
Bass, Henry	53rd	Infantry	Co. K
Bass, Jesse	102nd	Infantry	Co. K
Battie, Bird	105th	Infantry	Co. G
Battie, Mat	105th	Infantry	Co. G
Battle, Moses	55th	Infantry	Co. C
Battuse, Henry	118th	Infantry	Co. H
Bay, Lundy	81st	Infantry	Co. K
Bean, John	15th	Cavalry	Co. G
Beard, Henry	105th	Infantry	Co. A
Beasley, Brisber	102nd	Infantry	Co. F
Beasley, Edward/Edmond	58th	Infantry	Co. H, A
Beasley/Beazley, Charles	58th	Infantry	Co. D
Bebly, Green	19th	Infantry`	Co. F
Bedell, Bristol	124th	Infantry	Co. C
Bell, Charles	65th	Infantry	Co. G

Bell, Charles	56th	Infantry	Co. F
Bell, Jacob	4th	Cavalry	Co. C
Bell, Jacob	12th	Cavalry	Co. L
Bembine, John	118th	Infantry	Co. F
Berg, Cleve	57th	Infantry	Co. A
Berry, Alexander	13th	Cavalry	Co. A, K
Berry, Philip	34th	Infantry	Co. F
Berry, Thomas	129th	Infantry	Co. E
Bird, Benjamin	4th	Cavalry	Co. A
Bishop, Columbus	62nd	Infantry	Co. K
Black, Alfred	7th	Cavalry	Co. G
Black, Osker	7th	Cavalry	Co. G
Blair, Abraham	12th	Cavalry	Co. C
Blair, Reuben	50th	Infantry	Co. D
Blair, Lewis W.	10th	Infantry	Co. H
Bolen, John G.	2nd	Cavalry	Co. A
Booker, Irving	118th	Infantry	Co. B
Borain, Abram	95th	Infantry	Co. G
Bowen, John	43rd	Infantry	Co. K
Bowen, Manuel	43rd	Infantry	Co. K
Boyd, Henry	95th	Infantry	Co. G
Boyl, Tobias (Tob)	8th	Infantry	Co. I
Bracy, Charles	124th	Infantry	Co. K
Braden, Porter	50th	Infantry	Co. D
Brayden, Lymus	50th	Infantry	Co. H
Bramlet, Henry	66th	Infantry	Co. K
Branch, John	105th	Infantry	Co. F
Branch, John	105th	Infantry	Co. F
Breckenridge, Samuel	29th	Infantry	Co. D
Bridges, Cato	34th	Infantry	
Brinden, George	11th	Cavalry	Co. C
Bristol, George	58th	Infantry	Co. A
Britton, William	2nd	Cavalry	Co. K, B
Brooks, Jackson	72nd	Infantry	Co. D
Brown, Albert	56th	Infantry	Co. B
Brown, Charles	129th	Infantry	Co. K
Brown, Frank	7th	Cavalry	Co. B
Brown, Isaac	72nd	Infantry	Co. A
Brown, James	89th	Infantry	Co. E
Brown, Jim	59th	Infantry	Co. H
Brown, John	19th	Infantry	Co. H
Brown, John	43rd	Infantry	Co. E
Brown, John	50th	Infantry	Co. K
Brown, John	60th	Infantry	Co. E
Brown, John	118th	Infantry	Co. F

Brown, Milton	11th	Infantry	Co. C
Brown, Thomas	11th	Infantry	Co. U
Brown, William	129th	Infantry	Co. G
Bryan, Aleck	72nd	Infantry	Co. D
Bucey, Isan	7th	Cavalry	Co. I
Buck, Amos	111th	Infantry	Co. E
Bullock, Major	92nd	Infantry	Co. B
Bunkley, Solomon	118th	Infantry	Co. G
Bunton, Milton	129th	Infantry	Co. I
Burns, William	2nd	Lt. Atty	Battery F
Burrebeina, John	118th	Infantry	Co. C
Bute, Amos	48th	Infantry	Co. K
Butler, Benjamin	12th	Infantry	Co. C
Caesar, Julius	105th	Infantry	Co. H
Caldwell, Amos	52nd	Infantry	Co. D
Camel, William	56th	Infantry	Co. E
Campbell/Cambell, Cato	4th	Cavalry	Co. C
Campbell, Cato	12th	Cavalry	Co. L
Cambell, Marshall	92nd	Infantry	Co. E
Cannon, Miles	78th	Infantry	Co. H
Carr, William	7th	Infantry	Co. H
Carroll, Washington	12th	Infantry	Co. B
Carter, Dave	1st Lt. Arty. Battery.		Co. D
Carter, Jackson	93rd	Infantry	Co. H
Carter, James	7th	Infantry	Co. H
Carter, John	2nd	Lt. Atty.	Battery L
Carter, Peter	2nd	Cavalry	Co. F, A
Cary, Thomas	118th	Infantry	Co. K
Charlton, Robert	52nd	Infantry	Co. G
Chatman, Amos	2nd	Cavalry	Co. H, E
Childs, John	46th	Infantry	Co. D
Claiborne (Claburn), Arthur	(30) 46th	Infantry	Co. C
Clark, James	129th	Infantry	Co. C
Clark, George	17th	Infantry	Co. F
Clay, Henry	129th	Infantry	Co. G
Cohen, Perry	7th	Infantry	Co. A, B
Cole, Frank	18th	Infantry	Co. K
Collem, Horace	7th	Calvary	Co. K
Collins, John	9th	Infantry	Co. F
Collins, John	27th	Infantry	Co. K
Colman, Wyatt	124th	Infantry	Co. C
Colson, Sampson	43rd	Infantry	Co. F
Cook, Abraham	124th	Infantry	Co. A
Copeland, Samuel	129th	Infantry	Co A
Crawford, Thomas	95th	Infantry	Co. B

Cregg, John	56th	Infantry	Co. F
Crockett, Washington	7th	Cavalry	Co. I?
Cupid, Lem	95th	Infantry	Co. C
Daurity, Samuel	50th	Infantry	Co. F
Davidson, Augustus	13th	Cavalry	Co. D
Davidson, Tilton	46th	Infantry	Co. K
Davis, Charles	56th	Infantry	Co. B
Davis, Harry	95th	Infantry	Co. I
Davis, Robert	8th	Infantry	Co. G
Defoe, William	102nd	Infantry	Co. F
Denman, Riley	7th	Infantry	Co. H
Dickens, Cicero	46th	Infantry	Co. A
Dickens, Joshua	2nd	Cavalry	Co. H, E
Dickens, Stephen	92nd	Infantry	Co. K
Dickens, Bill	30th	Infantry	Co. A
Dickens, William	117th	Infantry	Co. I
Diggs, John	72nd	Infantry	Co. A
Dillahunt, James	111th Infantry transferred to 48th Infantry		Co. I
Dillon, Isaac	72nd	Infantry	Co. E
Dismuke, Jacob	102nd	Infantry	Co. G
Dodd, William	95th	Infantry	Co. H
Dorsey, Charles	72nd	Infantry	Co. I
Dosier, Joseph	20th	Infantry	Co. C
Douglas, Daniel	129th	Infantry	Co D
Douglas, John	129th	Infantry	
Douglass, Hezekiah Ford	95th	Infantry	Co. C
Dover, John	4th	Cavalry	Co. E
Drain, Robert	83rd	Infantry	Co. I
Edwards, John	19th	Infantry	Co. D
Edwards, John	60th	Infantry	Co. E
Elegant, George	62nd	Infantry	Co. A
Elic, Roseborough	117th	Infantry	Co. F
Ellison, Gansy	46th	Infantry	Co. C
Ellis, Henry	46th	Infantry	
Faulis, Henry	102nd	Infantry	Co. A
Feelin, Harrison	118th	Infantry	Co. E
Furguson, Edmond	83rd	Infantry	Co. B
Fields, John	2nd	Cavalry	Co. F, A
Fifer, Joseph	59th	Infantry	Co. E
Fisher, Wyatt	105th	Infantry	Co. K
Fitzgerald, John	72nd	Infantry	Co. C
Flack, John	59th	Infantry	
Flack, Tom	59th	Infantry	Co. H
Flake, George	111th Infantry transferred to 48th		Co. I
Floyd, Louis	57th	Infantry	Co. E

Foster, Haywood	66th	Infantry	Co. A
Franklin, Benjamin D.	72nd	Infantry	Co. A
Franklin, Benjamin	54th	Infantry	Co. G
Franklin, William	129th	Infantry`	Co. A
Ferguson, Matthew	95th	Infantry	Co. H
Gabriel, Eli	50th	Infantry	Co. I
Gardner, Cleveland	40th	Infantry	
Gardner, Cleveland	93rd	Infantry	Co. E
Gazaphall, Franklin	2nd	Cavalry	Co. K, B
Gibson, Saunders	57th	Infantry	Co. K
Gidwell, Jack	129th	Infantry	Co. E
Gilmore, Austin	111th	Infantry	Co. E
Golson, Samuel	83rd	Infantry	Co. B
Goodman, Richard S.	105th	Infantry	Co. C
Gordon, Cleveland	40th	Infantry	Co. K
Gordon, James	124th	Infantry	Co. D
Gordon, William	46th	Infantry	Co. K
Gordon, William	30th	Infantry	Co. K
Gould, William	124th	Infantry	Co. G
Grant, Charles	2nd	Cavalry	Co. F, A
Green, Boulon	118th	Infantry	Co. I
Green, Cook	11th	Infantry	Co. E
Green, Frank	13th	Cavalry	Co. D
Green, Gordon	78th	Infantry	Co. F
Green, Isum	8th	Infantry	Co. B
Green, James	56th	Infantry	Co. E
Green, John	11th	Cavalry	Co. E
Green, John	43rd	Infantry	Co. E
Green, Robert	81st	Infantry	Co. G
Grigsby, Martin	9th	Infantry	Co. H
Grisby, Charles	45th	Infantry	Co. A
Grixby, Burk/Buck	9th	Infantry	Co. F
Grummell, Samuel	59th	Infantry	Co. A
Hall, Charley	118th	Infantry	Co. B
Hall, Martin	50th	Infantry	Co. I
Hamilton, Henry	12th	Infantry	Co. G
Handerson, Leffert	43rd	Infantry	Co. E
Hanley, Fred	62nd	Infantry	Co. B
Hanner, Samuel	50th	Infantry	Co. D
Hanson, Bristol	58th	Infantry	Co. F
Hardy, Henry	56th	Infantry	Co. D
Harmon, Simon	81st	Infantry	Co. A
Harper, John	129th	Infantry	Co. F
Harper, Jordan	129th	Infantry	Co. F
Harris, Robert	19th	Infantry	Co. D

Harris, Robert	60th	Infantry	Co. A
Harrison, Feelen	118th	Infantry	Co. B
Harrison, William	72nd	Infantry	Co. G, H
Harrison, William Henry	19th	Infantry	Co. A
Harwood, John G.	18th	Infantry	Co. B
Hasty, James	56th	Infantry	Co. D
Harvel, Richard	79th	Infantry	
Hayes, Caroll	54th	Infantry	Co. H
Hays, Smith	72nd	Infantry	Co. C
Henderson, James	4th	Cavalry	Co. B
Henderson, James	12th	Cavalry	Co. I
Henderson, Thomas	72nd	Infantry	Co. E
Henderson, Thomas	12th	Infantry	Co. E
Herd, John	46th	Infantry	Co. D
Herdy, Riley	4th	Cavalry	Co. B
Herdy Riley	12th	Cavalry	Co. I
Herron, Benjamin	83rd	Infantry	Co. I
Hicks, John	2nd	Cavalry	Co. I
Higden, Andrew	50th	Infantry	Co. K
Hill, Ely	43rd	Infantry	Co. D
Hill, Green T.	66th	Infantry	Co. D
Hill, James	4th	Cavalry	Co. A
Hilliard, Dick	95th	Infantry	Co. F
Hobson, Mike	124th	Infantry	Co. I
Hogan, Alexander	10th	Infantry	Co. H
Holly George	81st	Infantry	Co. B
Houston, Martin	11th	Infantry	Co. H
Howard, Lot	57th	Infantry	Co. B
Hubbard, Guttrill	8th	Infantry	Co. A
Hudson, Gabe	46th	Infantry	Co. H
Hudson, Gilbert	118th	Infantry	Co. A
Hudson, Joshua	46th	Infantry	Co. H
Hudson, Peter	51st	Infantry	Co. E
Hurt, Richard	8th	Infantry	Co. B
Hurt, Richard	17th	Infantry	Co. C
Huston, Andrew	66th	Infantry	Co. D
Ingam, Daniel	18th	Infantry	Co. I
Jack, Christopher	118th	Infantry	Co. E
Jackson, Charles	12th	Infantry	Co. H
Jackson, Jerry	72nd	Infantry	Co. D
Jackson, Matthew	102nd	Infantry	Co. B
Jackson, William	7th	Infantry	Co. B
Jacobs, Abram	18th	Infantry	Co. G
James, John	60th	Infantry	Co. F
Jefferson, Albert	10th	Infantry	Co. B

Jefferson, Horace	45th	Infantry	Co. K
Jennings, Richard	111th Infantry transferred to 48th		Co. H
Johnson, Albert	102nd	Infantry	Co. C
Johnson, Augustus	4th	Cavalry	Co. C
Johnson, Bill	58th	Infantry	Co. B
Johnson, Felix	40th	Infantry	Co. K
Johnson, Jordan	77th	Infantry	Co. C
Johnson, Joseph	124th	Infantry	Co. B
Johnson, Thomas	29th	Infantry	Co. C
Johnson, William	51st	Infantry	Co. E
Johnston, Augustus	12th	Cavalry	Co. L
Jones, Elias	118th	Infantry	Co. D
Jones, George	4th	Cavalry	Co. C
Jones, George	12th	Cavalry	Co. L
Jones, James	62nd	Infantry	Co. F
Jones, Jordan	72nd	Infantry	Co. G
Jones, Lucien	62nd	Infantry	Co. B
Jones, Nat	4th	Cavalry	Co. B
Jones, Paul	30th	Infantry	Co. C
Jones, Robert	105th	Infantry	Co. D
Jones, Stephen	95th	Infantry	Co. C
Jones, Thomas	28th	Infantry	Co. A
Jones, William	19th	Infantry	Co. D
Kelly, Henry	95th	Infantry	Co. E
King, Henry	48th	Infantry	Co. D
Knowles, Henry	4th	Cavalry	Co. A
Lamar, Peter	15th	Cavalry	Co. B
Lee, Buck	66th	Infantry	Co. H
Lee, Henry	72nd	Infantry	Co. I
Lee, James	118th	Infantry	Co. E
Lewis, Emanuel	57th	Infantry	Co. K
Lightfoot, Benjamin	18th	Infantry	Co. E
Lightfoot, Marion	54th	Infantry	Co. G
Link, Robert	105th	Infantry	Co. B
Long, Jerry	12th	Infantry	Co. I
Long, William	12th	Infantry	Co. G
Lucas, John	81st	Infantry	Co. C
Lunda, Bay	50th	Infantry	Co. K
Lymus, Brayden	50th	Infantry	Co. H
Mack, Ed	2nd	Cavalry	Co. I
Madison, Coriolanus	24th	Infantry	Co. A
Maguire, George	129th	Infantry	Co. I
Malvin, Robert	124th	Infantry	Co. G
Manningcar, Addison	57th	Infantry	Co. E
Mars, Frank	54th	Infantry	Co. A

Mason, Peter	118th Infantry transferred to 48th Infantry		Co. F
McAlpine, Caesar	124th	Infantry	Co. A
McClellan, Henry	57th	Infantry	Co. E
McCord, Benjamin	65th	Infantry	Co. G
McCullough, William	60th	Infantry	Co. D
McGrew, Joseph	124th	Infantry	Co. E
McKeal, Clayborn	72nd	Infantry	Co. F
McLauren, Anderson	50th	Infantry	Co. E
McLean, Thomas	124th	Infantry	Co. D
McLelian, Nash	34th	Infantry	
Mead, Aleck	4th	Cavalry	Co. E
Meshack, Thomas	118th	Infantry	Co. A
Metcalf, Oscar	118th	Infantry	Co. G
Miles, Elijah	91st	Infantry	Co. K
Miller, John D.	118th	Infantry	Co. G
Miller, Wesley	118th	Infantry`	Co. C
Milton, Assa	72nd	Infantry	Co. F
Minor, William	72nd	Infantry	Co. F
Mitchell, Lewis	30th	Infantry	Co. H
Mitchell, Steve	58th	Infantry	Co. B
Moran, William	12th	Infantry	Co. B
Monroe, Madison	95th	Infantry	Co. A
Morrison, David	50th	Infantry	Co. F
Morse, Maurice	72nd	Infantry	Co. A
Moses, Dowell	117th	Infantry	Co. F
Mullin, William	77th	Infantry	Co. G
Mullin, William	103rd	Infantry	Co. B
Mumford, Henry	83rd	Infantry	Co. K
Nelson, John	57th	Infantry	Co. A
Noah, Alexander	34th	Infantry	Co. A
Noble, Edward	83rd	Infantry	Co. F
Nowles, Lewis	124th	Infantry	Co. B
Oakes, Stephen	7th	Cavalry	Co. L
Olmsted, Arthur	12th	Infantry	Co. I
Olmsted, Dudley	12th	Infantry	Co. I
Osborn, Thomas	118th	Infantry	Co. B
Ousley, John	124th	Infantry	Co. G
Owens, Jesse	124th	Infantry	Co. G
Owens, Stephen	129th	Infantry	Co. F
Parker, Cornelius	4th	Cavalry	Co. A
Parker, Moses	103rd	Infantry	Co. B
Parmil, William	81st	Infantry	Co. C
Paulk, Robert	7th	Infantry	Co. B
Pearce, Frank	60th	Infantry	Co. A
Peck, Major	57th	Infantry	Co. E

Pennybaker, James	102nd	Infantry	Co. I
Perkins, Tillman	105th	Infantry	Co. B
Phillips, Berry	34th	Infantry	
Pierce, Frank	19th	Infantry	Co. C
Piper, Hillyard	124th	Infantry	Co. A
Polk, Peter	105th	Infantry	Co. H
Pollard, Frank	11th	Infantry	Co. E
Preston, Jackson	98th	Infantry	Co. H
Pompon, Alexander	118th	Infantry	Co. C
Posey, Jubilee	31st	Infantry	Co. K
Powell, Alexander	48th	Infantry	Co. A, F
Powell, Allen	81st	Infantry	Co. F
Pratt, Arnold	118th	Infantry	Co. D
Prewett (Pruit), Thomas	59th	Infantry	
Price, Orris	129th	Infantry	Co. H
Prior, Middleton	57th	Infantry	Co. I
Providence, Peter	95th	Infantry	Co. K
Pruitt, Thomas	59th	Infantry	Co. D
Putnam, Edward	2nd	Cavalry	Co. K, B
Ralston, Ephraim	102nd	Infantry	Co. K
Ramer, Peter	12th	Infantry	Co. F
Ramsey, Abraham	35th	Infantry	Co. F
Ramsbury, Robert E.	124th	Infantry	Co. E
Randall, William	118th	Infantry	Co. B
Reedus, Morgan	12th	Infantry	Co. K
Reese, Zenon	118th	Infantry	Co. C
Reynolds, Richard	48th	Infantry	Co. D
Reynolds, Jasper	10th	Infantry	Co. C
Reynolds, Shadrack	7th	Infantry	Co. K
Roberts, Isaac	117th	Infantry	Co. A
Roberts, William	62nd	Infantry	Co. G
Rodgers, William	48th	Infantry	Co. D
Rogan, James	102nd	Infantry	Co. G
Rone, Daniel	93rd	Infantry	Co. G
Ross, Albert	72nd	Infantry	Co. H
Runnel, Spencer	57th	Infantry	Co. E
Russell, Henry	102nd	Infantry	Co. E
Samuel, Sampson	59th	Infantry	Co. F
Schadrick, Bill	58th	Infantry	Co. A
Scott, Thomas	2nd	Cavalry	Co. H, E
Scott, William	118th	Infantry	Co. G
Shades, Albert	124th	Infantry	Co. A
Shaw, Henry	11th	Cavalry	Co. K
Sheridan, Henry S.	124th	Infantry	Co. D
Simmons, Hosea	45th	Infantry	Co. K

Name	Regiment	Branch	Company
Simms, James	124th	Infantry	Co. E
Simons, Moses	45th	Infantry	Co. G
Simpson, Jefferson	7th	Infantry	Co. K
Skoggs, Frank	48th	Infantry	Co. B
Smith, Hiram	12th	Infantry	Co. B
Smith, James R.	72nd	Infantry	Co. B
Smith, Jesse	118th	Infantry	Co. E
Smith, Levi	48th	Infantry	Co. F
Smith, Rolla D.	50th	Infantry	Co. A
Smith, Samuel	50th	Infantry	Co. G
Smith, Tony	6th	Cavalry	Co. M
Sneed, Ezekiah	12th	Infantry	Co. K
Spencer, Samuel	2nd	Cavalry	Co. I
Stapleton, Steiger	83rd	Infantry	Co. F
Steel, Green	48th	Infantry	Co. B
Stevens, Alexander	78th	Infantry	Co. A
Stewart, Alexander	50th	Infantry	Co. E
Stratton, Stewart	(50th? 81st	Infantry	Co. I
Sullivan, Israel	62nd	Infantry	Co. F
Swinney, Jorden	6th	Cavalry	Co. M
Talbot, Ike	13th	Cavalry	Co. A, K
Taylor, Abner	18th	Infantry	Co. I
Taylor, Benjamin	4th	Cavalry	Co. B
Taylor, Britton	8th	Infantry	Co. B
Taylor, Britton	17th	Infantry	Co. G
Taylor, Elijah	(46th?) 30th	Infantry	Co. C
Taylor, Henry C.	18th	Infantry	Co. B
Taylor, Jim	9th	Infantry	Co. C, F
Taylor, Reuben	124th	Infantry	Co. E
Taylor, Rice	10th	Infantry	Co. C
Taylor, Wylie	118th	Infantry	Co. H
Tedwell, John	18th Infantry transferred to 48th Infantry		Co. G
Tedwell, Thornton	18th Infantry transferred to 48th Infantry		Co. G
Tefler, James	62nd	Infantry	Co. G
Temple, William	62nd	Infantry	Co. G
Tennessee, John	62nd	Infantry	Co. A
Thomas, John	55th	Infantry	Co. D
Thompson, William	118th	Infantry	Co. K
Thornson, Jackson	66th	Infantry	Co. D
Tibbs, Elias	124th	Infantry	Co. E
Tinley, Michael	87th	Infantry	Co. F
Toliver, George	8th	Infantry	Co. E
Toliver, Ned	98th	Infantry	Co. B
Torian, Archy	42nd	Infantry	Co. K
Tucker, George	118th Infantry transferred to 48th Infantry		Co. G

Name	Regiment	Branch	Company
Tucker, William	130th	Infantry	Co. C
Turner, Anthony	7th	Cavalry	Co. F
Turner, Hanibal	12th	Infantry	Co. G
Turner, Leroy	30th	Infantry	Co. A
Udley, Lee	18th	Infantry	Co. A
Van Donelson	43rd	Infantry	Co. C
Vickers, James	118th	Infantry	Co. I
Wade, Charley	81st	Infantry	Co. G
Walker, George	43rd	Infantry	Co. A
Walker, John	102nd	Infantry	Co. C
Wallace, Toby M.	118th	Infantry	Co. C
Walton, William	129th	Infantry	Co. B
Warner, John	12th	Infantry	Co. E
Warner, Preston	89th	Infantry	Co. H
Warren, Cornelius	12th	Infantry	Co. A
Warren, Major	12th	Infantry (transf. to USCT) teamster	
Warren, Patrick	12th	Infantry	Co. C
Washington, Aaron	57th	Infantry	Co. D
Washington, George	4th	Cavalry	Co. E
Washington, George	10th	Infantry	Co. G
Washington, George	53rd	Infantry	Co. C
Washington, George	55th	Infantry	Co. K
Washington, George	66th	Infantry	Co. D
Washington, George	72nd	Infantry	Co. I
Washington, George	81st	Infantry	Co. D
Washington, George	118th	Infantry	Co. C
Washington, George	124th	Infantry	Co. B
Watkins, Albert G.	22nd	Infantry	Co B
Watkins, Henry	95th	Infantry	Co. A
Watson, Manuel	62nd	Infantry	Co. F
Watson, Robert	34th	Infantry	
Weatherly, Alfred	46th	Infantry	Co. B
Wells, Richard	45th	Infantry	Co. G
West, Peter	66th	Infantry	Co. A
Weston, John	72nd	Infantry	Co. F
White, Charles	45th	Infantry	Co. A
White, Daniel	66th	Infantry	Co. G
White, Philip H.	92nd	Infantry	Co. K
White, Thomas	50th	Infantry	Co. G
White, Thomas	9th	Infantry	Co. C teamster
Wiley, Emroy	20th	Infantry	Co. A
Wilkes, Abraham	18th	Infantry	Co. I
Wilkins, Henry	2nd	Cavalry	Co. K, B

?Williams, George		9th	Infantry	Co. E
Williams, George		118th	Infantry	Co. E
Williams, Henry		72nd	Infantry	Co. K
Williams, Isaac		124th	Infantry	Co. I
Williams, James		11th	Cavalry	Co. C
Williams, Zachariah		81st	Infantry	Co. F
Wilson, Fonrose		10th	Infantry	Co. B
Wilson, Wesley		83rd	Infantry	Co. K
Winters, Edward		13th	Cavalry	Co. D
Winters, Henry		124th	Infantry	Co. D
Wood, Thomas		83rd	Infantry	Co. A
Woodford, John		72nd	Infantry	Co. C
Woods, Joseph		72nd	Infantry	Co. E
Woodson, Henry		66th	Infantry	Co. A
Wooley, Edward		12th	Infantry	Co. K

☆**INDIANA**

Abernathy, George		66th	Infantry	Co. C
Abernathy, Reuben		66th	Infantry	Co. D
Allen, John		7th	Cavalry	Co. D
Barnett, George		44th	Infantry	Co. H
Brown, Elias		44th	Infantry	Co. A
Brown, E.		74th	Infantry	Co. A
Brown, Isaac		7th	Cavalry	Co. A, C
Jones, Eli		22nd	Infantry	Co. D
Jones, Eli	(82nd?)	74th	Infantry	Co. I
Jones, Elias		82nd	Infantry	Co. D
Jones, Frank		66th	Infantry	Co. I
Jones, George		82nd	Infantry	Co. G
Jones, Green		22nd	Infantry	Co. E
Jones, Green		82nd	Infantry	Co C
Melelian, Nash		78th	Infantry	Co. G
Miles, Cannon		78th	Infantry	Co. G
Miles, Cannon		34th	Infantry	
Miller, Elijah		72nd	Infantry	Co. A
Miller, Turner		44th	Infantry	Co. E
Moon, David		13th	Cavalry	Co. I
Monroe, Madison		95th	Infantry	Co. A
Rodgers, Green		22nd	Infantry	Co. D
Rodgers, Green		82nd	Infantry	Co. D
Smith, Nelson		44th	Infantry	Co. D
Smith, Nelson		72nd	Infantry	Co. G
Turner, Thomas		8th	Infantry	Co. C

Washington, George	15th	Infantry	Co. C
Washington, George	25th	Infantry	Co. D
Washington, George	26th	Infantry	Co. F
Washington, George	46th	Infantry	Co. H
Watson, Robert	78th	Infantry	Co. I
Watson, Robert	34th	Infantry	
White, John L.	44th	Infantry	Co. D
White, John L.	72nd	Infantry	Co. D

☆IOWA

Anderson, Peter	34th	Infantry	Co. K
Ashby, William	34th	Infantry	Co. I
Ashby, William	38th	Infantry	Co. B, I
Johnson, Peter	38th	Infantry	Co. K

☆KANSAS

Alexander, George	1st	Infantry	Co. B
Allen, Solomon	8th	Infantry	Co. I
Armstad, Henry	1st	Infantry	Co. F
Barrett, Isam	1st	Infantry	Co. B
Beck, Lewis	Lt. Atty.		2nd Ind. Btty.
Beck, Lewis	Lt. Atty.		3rd Ind. Btty.
Beck, Samuel	Lt. Atty.		2nd Ind. Btty.
Beck, Samuel	Lt. Atty.		3rd Ind. Btty.
Bell, Thomas	8th	Infantry	Co. F
Bennett, Tip	1st	Infantry	Co. G
Berry, Ward	Lt. Atty.	Infantry	3rd Ind. Btty.
Boone, Daniel	14th	Cavalry	Co. G
Burl, William	1st	Infantry	Co. G
Calvin, James	1st	Infantry	Co. H
Carthur, George	1st	Infantry	Co. F
Clay, Henry	1st	Infantry	Co. G
Collins, Thomas	16th	Cavalry	Co. G
Collins, Thomas (Tom)	1st	Cavalry	Co. K
Daniel, Michael	1st	Infantry	Co. C
Dickson, Bryan	1st	Infantry	Co. H
Dow, Miller	1st	Infantry	Co. C
Elder, Robert	1st	Infantry	Co. K
Ewing, Fleming	11th	Cavalry	Co. B
Farris, Henry	8th	Infantry	Co. H
Gabriel, Benjamin	1st	Infantry	Co. F
Gaines, Andrew	14th	Cavalry	Co. C

Gibbons, Carroll	1st	Infantry	Co. H
Gibbons, Riley	1st	Infantry	Co. H
Gibson, Piahmond	1st	Infantry	Co, A, B
Giton, Henry	1st	Infantry	Co. K
Graham, Harrison	8th	Infantry	Co. F
Gregor, William	1st	Infantry	Co. H
Hemperton, John	1st	Infantry	Co. I
Henman, James	1st	Infantry	????
Hester, John	16th	Cavalry	Co. G
Hester, John	1st	Infantry	Co. B
Jackson, Andrew	8th	Infantry	Co. H
Johnston, George	1st	Infantry	Co. E
Jones, Dick	1st	Infantry	Co. C
Jones, Willis	15th	Cavalry	Co. B
Lalter, Jordan	1st	Infantry	Co. B
Lane, Stephen	11th	Cavalry	Co. K
Lee, James A.	11th	Cavalry	Co. M
McLean, Arthur	1st	Infantry	Co. B, G
Mitchell, Fryday	1st	Infantry	Co. F
Miles, Isaac	1st	Infantry	Co. H, B
Moore, William	14th	Cavalry	Co. D
Murry, Caleb	1st	Infantry	Co. F
Newman, James	1st	Infantry	Co. E
Oliver, Hamilton	1st	Infantry	Co. D
Pebles, George	1sr	Infantry	Co. D
Porter, James	11th	Cavalry	Co. K
Powell, Nathan	14th	Cavalry	Co. D
Ramsey, Douglas	1st	Infantry	Co. A
Richardson, Dick	16th	Cavalry	Co. G
Richardson, Dick	1st	Infantry	Co. G
Ripley, Joseph	1st	Infantry	Co. G
Roberson, Andrew	1st	Infantry	Co. D
Sanders, Calein (Calvin)	1st	Infantry	Co. E
Sanders, Simon	Lt. Atty		2nd Ind. Btty
Sanders, Simon	Lt. Atty.		3rd Ind. Btty.
Sharp, Robert	1st	Infantry	Co. E
Shook, Edward	8th	Infantry	Co. A
Shook, Isaac	8th	Infantry	Co. A
Sisson, Silas	1st	Infantry	Co. E
Smith, Dandy	1st	Infantry	Co. I
Smith, Horace	1st	Infantry	Co. G
Snoddy, Jerimiah	5th	Cavalry	Co. L
Speer, Albert G.	7th	Cavalry	Co. A
Stanley, Rufus	1st	Infantry	Co. A
Todd, John	1st	Infantry	Co. H

Vaughn, Gabriel	16th	Cavalry	Co. G
Vaughn, Gabriel	1st	Infantry	Co. K
Viley, Charles	1st	Infantry	Co. F
Wade, David	1st	Infantry	Co. K
Washington, George	8th	Infantry	Co. A
Whitey, Solimon	1st	Infantry	Co. B
Williams, Alfred	1st	Infantry	Co. F
Williams, Alonzo	1st	Infantry	Co. B
Williams, Gilbert	8th	Infantry	Co. K
Wilson, D.	1st	Infantry	Co. D
Young, Berry	1st	Infantry	Co. I

☆KENTUCKY

Washington, George	28th	Infantry	Co. C

☆LOUISIANA

Abraham, Sidney	1st	Cavalry	Co. D
Allison, James	1st	Infantry	Co. K
Austin, Charles	1st	Infantry	Co. K
Barkman, Peter	1st	Cavalry	Co. A
Bradley, Henry	1st	Cavalry	Co. A
Brown, Henry	1st	Infantry	Co. B
Brown, Henry	1st	New Orleans Inf.	Co. B
Brown, Jackson	1st	Cavalry	Co. A
Brown, James	1st	Cavalry	Co. D
Brown, Joseph	1st	Cavalry	Co. C
Brown, Kirby	1st	Cavalry	Co. G
Brown, Parker	1st	Cavalry	Co. E
Clay, Henry	1st	Cavalry	Co. F
Davis, John	1st	New Orleans Inf.	Co. A
Davis, John	1st	Infantry	Co. A
Davis, Joseph	1st	Infantry	Co. D
Dimon, Samuel	1st	Infantry	Co. K
Ely, Joseph	1st	Infantry	Co. G
Frost, Henry	1st	Cavalry	Co. G
Hall, Benjamin	1st	Cavalry	Co. F
Hays, George	1st	Cavalry	Co. A
Hilliard, Jackson	1st	Cavalry	Co. A
Jackson, Charles	1st	New Orleans Inf.	Co. D
Jackson, Charles	1st	Infantry	Co. I
Jackson, Isaac	1st	Cavalry	Co. A

Johnson, Henry	1st	Infantry	Co. C
Johnson, Henry	1st	New Orleans Inf.	Co. C
Johnson, John	1st	Infantry	Co. I
Johnson, John	1st	New Orleans Inf.	Co. H
Johnson, Thomas	1st	Cavalry	Co. A
King, Joseph	1st	Infantry	Co. H
King, Joseph	1st	New Orleans Inf.	Co. E
Martin, Oscar	1st	Cavalry	Co. K
Miner, Charles	1st	Cavalry	Co. D
Roche, David	1st	Infantry	Co. C
Sheppard, Edward	1st	New Orleans Inf.	Co. E
Sheppard, Edward	1st	Infantry	Co. F
Smith, Claiborne	1st	Cavalry	Co. B
Smith, James	1st	Infantry	Co. K
Squash, John	1st	Infantry	Co. E
Squash, John	1st	New Orleans Inf.	Co. A
Tost, Henry	1st	Cavalry	
Warwick, David	1st	Infantry	Co. I
Washington, Henry	1st	Cavalry	Co. G
Wells, Moses	1st	Cavalry	Co. I
Welsley, Henry	1st	Cavalry	Co. B
Welsley, Frederick	1st	Cavalry	Co. G
White, Robert	1st	Infantry	Co. H
White, Robert	1st	New Orleans Inf.	Co. H
Williams, James	1st	Infantry	Co. A
Williams, James	1st	New Orleans Inf.	Co. A
Williams, Joseph	1st	Cavalry	Co. I
Young, Charles	1st	Cavalry	Co. I, E

☆MAINE

Barney, Marcellus	15th	Infantry	Co. B
Black, James	9th	Infantry	Co. K
Blake, Domingo	8th	Infantry	Co. E
Boles, Samuel	13th	Infantry	Co. I
Boles, Samuel	30th	Infantry	Co. I, A
Chisholm, John	8th	Infantry	Co. G
Dozier, Anthony	8th	Infantry	Co. K
Farley, Alfred	13th	Infantry	Co. C
Farley, Alfred	30th	Infantry	Co. K
Fields, January	8th	Infantry	Co. E
Furguson, Jim	8th	Infantry	Co. D
George, James	13th	Infantry	Co. K
George, James	30th	Infantry	Co. K

Gibbins, Gabiel	8th	Infantry	Co. I
Grant, Jacob	8th	Infantry	Co. F
Grant, Joseph	8th	Infantry	Co. G
Grate, Mark	8th	Infantry	Co. E
Green, Lyman	8th	Infantry	Co. G
Green, Nat	13th	Infantry	Co. F
Hamilton, Abraham	8th	Infantry	Co. F
Hayward, Bristol	8th	Infantry	Co. F
Henderson, Benjamin	13th	Infantry	Co. B
Henderson, Benjamin	30th	Infantry	Co. H
Hines, Richard	15th	Infantry	Co. B
Hugh, John	8th	Infantry	Co. C
Jackson, Samuel	1st	Cavalry	Co. F
Jenkins, John	8th	Infantry	Co. D
Jenkins, Stephen	8th	Infantry	Co. D
Johnson, Jacob	8th	Infantry	Co. A
Legree, Richard	8th	Infantry	Co. K
Lewis, William	8th	Infantry	Co. B
Mason, Wesley	13th	Infantry	Co. A, E
Mason, Wesley	30th	Infantry	Co. B
McDonald, Horace	13th	Infantry	Co. I
McKnight, Ellis	8th	Infantry	Co. E
Meigs, Thomas	13th	Infantry	Co. A
Mikes, Charles	8th	Infantry	Co. C
Miller, George	13th	Infantry	Co. C
Mitchel, David	9th	Infantry	Co. A
Price, Edwin	8th	Infantry	Co. B
Purchase, Hector	8th	Infantry	Co. B
Riley, Stephen	8th	Infantry	Co. B
Robinson, Peter	13th	Infantry	Co. F
Scott, Harry	8th	Infantry	Co. E
Scippio	8th	Infantry	Co. D
Simmons, William E.	13th	Infantry	Co. I
Smith, Joseph	8th	Infantry	Co. B
Smith, Leander	13th	Infantry	Co. E, A
Spencer, John	8th	Infantry	Co. H
Stelman, Peooher	12th	Infantry	
Sterns, Frank	13th	Infantry	Co. B
Stewart, John	13th	Infantry	Co. E
Torpin, Isaac	15th	Infantry	Co. E
Tyre, Ned	13th	Infantry	Co. H
Williamson, Paul	30th	Infantry	Co. B

☆MARYLAND

Brotten, John	8th	Infantry	Co. K
Devall, Richard	2nd	Infantry	Co. G
Harris, L.	8th	Infantry	Co. K
Robinson, Henry	2nd	Infantry	Co. G

☆MASSACHUSETTS

Allen, Washington	3rd	Cavalry	Co. A
Andrews, Andrew	17th	Infantry	Co. A
Andrews, George	17th	Infantry	Co. A
Bennett, Joseph	56th	Infantry	Co. B
Bibbins, Anthony	30th	Infantry	Co. H
Brown, Dease	4th	Calvary	Co. L
Brown, Leighton	56th	Infantry	Co. I
Brown, Solomon	30th	Infantry	Co. E
Butler, William	3rd	Cavalry	Co. I, E
Calhoun, Caleb	32nd	Infantry	Co. A, K
Chaplin, Moses	4th	Cavalry	Co. K
Clark, Frank	3rd	Cavalry	Co. C
Collins, William	3rd	Cavalry	Co. F, E, M
Cook, Eli	3rd	Cavalry	Co. I
Darden, Jonas	1st	Cavalry	Co. I
Darden, Jonas	4th	Cavalry	Co. A, I
Dease, Bram	1st	Cavalry	Co. L
Dease, Bram	4th	Cavalry	Co. L
Dotson, Thomas	31st	Infantry	Co. E
Elderkin, J. Russell	58th	Infantry	Co. C
Evans, Richard	3rd	Cavalry	Co. C
Godfrey, James	1st	Cavalry	Co. I
Golding, Berry	30th	Infantry	Co. F
Green, Henry	3rd	Cavalry	Co G
Haines, David	3rd	Cavalry	Co. H, F, M
Hains, Henry	3rd	Cavalry	Co. F
Halsey, John	3rd	Cavalry	Co. L, D, K
Harrison, George	(38th?) 30th	Infantry	Co. C
Harrison, Henry	31st	Infantry	Co. F, H, D
Haupt, Henry	31st	Infantry	Co. G
Henderson, William	26th	Infantry	Co. B
Henderson, William	38th	Infantry	Co. D
Jackson, Edward	31st	Infantry	Co. K
Lee, William	26th	Infantry	
Lee, Wilson	38th	Infantry	Co. E

Marcus, Frank	31st	Infantry	Co. B, A, K
Phillips, Lewis	3rd	Cavalry	Co. M
Potter, Allic	30th	Infantry	Co. K
Powers, Dick	3rd	Cavalry	Co. F
Rice, Frank	31st	Infantry	Co. G
Sands, Robert H.	38th	Infantry	Co. B
Scott, Burrill	31st	Infantry	Co. G, C
Seabrook, Ansel	1st	Cavalry	Co. L
Seabrook, Ansel	4th	Cavalry	Co. L
Semmes, Joseph	3rd	Cavalry	Co. D
Shelby, Maddison	31st	Infantry	Co. E
Small, Stephen	1st	Cavalry	Co. K
?Thompson, John	24th	Infantry	
Thompson, Peter	3rd	Cavalry	Co. M
Wells, William	Lt. Arty.	6th Ind. Battery	
Wilder, Gansey	30th	Infantry	Co. H
Williams, Peter	31st	Infantry	Co. D, I
Woodlow, Henry	26th	Infantry	Co. E
Younger, Joseph	30th	Infantry	Co. K

☆**MICHIGAN**

Aikens, Ephriam	3rd	Cavalry	Co. B
Balfour, John M.	13th	Infantry	Co. K
Berry, Reuben	3rd	Cavalry	Co. A
Bird, Eldred	19th	Infantry	Co. E
Body, Isaac	3rd	Cavalry	Co. H
Braden, Charles	1st Lt. Art'y		Batt'y B
Brown, Frank	4th	Infantry	Co. D
Brown, Joseph	4th	Infantry	Co. D
Brown, William	6th	Cavalry	Co. C
Burrell, George	3rd	Cavalry	Co. K
Carroll, ?	18th	Infantry	Co. H
Crosby, Burton	18th	Infantry	Co. A
Dart, Thomas	9th	Infantry	Co. H
Davisison, Syrous	3rd	Cavalry	Co. A
Dickings, Samuel	3rd	Cavalry	Co. L
Duncan, Alfred	19th	Infantry	Co. H
Duncan, Harrison	19th	Infantry	Co. H
East, George	3rd	Cavalry	Co. B
Fox, William Dudley	2nd	Cavalry	Co. F
Guy, Benjamin F.	16th	Infantry	Co F
Hall, William	19th	Infantry	Co. I
Harden, William	1st Lt. Art'y		Batt'y B

Henry, Peter	9th	Infantry	Co. G
Hill, Joseph	18th	Infantry	Co. H
Hill, Morgan	18th	Infantry	Co. D
Lathrum, Henry	1st Lt. Art'y		Batt'y H
Lett, Aquilla	13th	Infantry	Co. M
Mason, George F.	8th	Cavalry	Co. B
Moore, William	13th	Infantry	Co. K
Pancha, John	3rd	Cavalry	Co. F
Parrish, Caleb	4th	Cavalry	Co. I
Payton, ?	19th	Infantry	Co. B
Pride, Jerry	3rd	Cavalry	Co. C
Richards, John	3rd	Cavalry	Co. H
Robinson, Joseph	1st Lt. Art'y		Batt'y E
Scott, George	3rd	Cavalry	
Sherod, Bob	3rd	Cavalry	Co. M
Shields, James	6th Hvy. Art'y		Co. G
Showell, Shadriac	9th	Infantry	Co. C
Smith, Jacob	10th	Cavalry	Co. F
Stone, Jacob	19th	Infantry	Co. F
Sweet, Prince	3rd	Cavalry	Co. I
Telles, James	19th	Infantry	Co. G
Telles, Jonathan	19th	Infantry	Co. G
Thomas, William	19th	Infantry	Co. D
Vincent, George	3rd	Cavalry	Co. H
Washington, Benjamin	19th	Infantry	Co. D
Washington, George	9th	Infantry	Co. E
Weaver, Tom	3rd	Cavalry	Co. M
West, Hopkins	13th	Infantry	Co. K
Wethington, Abraham	19th	Infantry	Co. D
Wilson, Peter	3rd	Cavalry	Co. C
Wilson, William	3rd	Cavalry	Co. C

☆MINNESOTA

Armstead, William M.	2nd	Cavalry	
Brown, Barney	5th	Infantry	Co. A
Butler, Lewis	3rd	Infantry	Co. I
Chambers, George	4th	Infantry	Co. K
Custer, William	3rd	Infantry	Co. G
Evans, Benjamin	1st	Hvy. Art'y.	Co. E
Faultner, Louis	3rd	Infantry	Co. D
Granville, Jack	3rd	Infantry	Co. C
Hawkins, Coleman	3rd	Infantry	Co. E
Hays, Joseph	3rd	Infantry	Co. C

Johnson, Joe	4th	Infantry	Co. G
Kimmens, Elijah	4th	Infantry	Co. A
Knowles, John	3rd	Infantry	Co. F
Lane, Dick	Lt. Att'y.		1st Ind. Batt'y
Martin, Prince	5th	Infantry	Co. I
Moseby, John	3rd	Infantry	Co. K
Saunders, Ned	3rd	Infantry	Co. B
Thomson, Richard	4th	Infantry	Co. H
Watson, Allen W.	2nd	Cavalry	Co. G
Wesley, John	3rd	Infantry	Co. D
White, William	1st	Hvy. Art'y.	Co. A
Wilburne, Milton	Lt. Att'y.		1st Ind. Btt'y

☆**MISSOURI**

Adams, James	18th	Infantry	Co. F
Adams, John	2nd	Lt. Art'y.	Btt'y I
Alfred, James	8th	Infantry	Co. F
Anderson, Jacob	1st	Cavalry	Co. K
Anderson, Jacob	7th	Cavalry	Co. I
Aron, Marion	24th	Infantry	Co. H
Arthur, John	7th	Infantry	Co. K
Arthur, John	11th	Infantry	Co. B
Atkins, Hilliard	6th	Infantry	Co. C
Baker, John	18th	Infantry	Co. C
Ball, John	21st	Infantry	Co. H
Ballantine, Columbus	18th	Infantry	Co. A
Barrow, Reuben	11th	Cavalry	Co. F
Beck, Samuel	1st	Lt. Art'y.	Btt'y K
Benton, William H.	11th	Cavalry	Co. G
Blackbon, Jefferson	8th	Infantry	Co. K
Blakeman, Allen	21st	Infantry	Co. I
Blow, Thomas	18th	Infantry	Co. I
Booker, James	8th	Infantry	Co. A
Bowman, Pompey	7th	Infantry	Co. E
Boyd, William	30th	Infantry	Co. B
Boiscoe, Mason	11th	Cavalry	Co. C
Boiscoe, Mason	3rd	Cavalry	Co. K, B
Broocks, Wesley	8th	Infantry	Co. K
Brooks, Samuel	7th	Cavalry	Co. K
Brown, James	2nd	Lt. Art'y.	Btt'y C
Brown, James	21st	Infantry	Co. G
Brown, Nat	11th	Cavalry	Co. E
Burnett, Cage	2nd	Lt. Art'y.	Btt'y M

Bush, Charles	23rd	Infantry	Co. F
Byers, James	24th	Infantry	Co. G, D
Calvin, John	31st	Infantry	Co. D
Calvin, John	32nd	Infantry (New Org.)	Co. A, E
Carney, Greene	24th	Infantry	Co. C
Carter, Alexander	8th	Infantry	Co. K
Clark, Marshall	31st	Infantry	Co. F
Clinton, Henry	West Eng. Reg.	Volunteers	Co. K
Collins, Hanson	24th	Infantry	Co. E
Conel, John	27th	Infantry	Co. H
Cramer, William	1st	St. Mil. Cavalry	Co. C
Daniel, Parish	21st	Infantry	Co. I
Davis, Doctor	21st	Infantry	Co. I
Dean, David	2nd	Lt. Arty.	Btty K
Dickerson, Ruben	8th	Infantry	Co. A
Dixon, Thomas	7th	Infantry	Co. B
Edwards, William	21st	Infantry	Co. I
Evans, Harry/Henry	18th	Infantry	Co. K
Evans, James	6th	Cavalry	Co. G
Floyd, Rush	7th	Cavalry	Co. D
Floyd, Rush	1st	Cavalry	Co. D
Gray, Milton	10th	Cavalry	Co. C
Green, Burch	7th	Infantry	Co. D
Green, John	7th	Infantry	Co. D
Griffin, Monroe	10th	Infantry	Co. D
Harris, James	1st	Cavalry	Co. H
Hestel, Samuel	10th	Cavalry	Co. K
Hicks, William	21st	Infantry	Co. F
Holt, Bucker	26th	Infantry	Co. D
Hunt, Nelson	25th	Infantry	
Hunter, Robert	21st	Infantry	Co. A
Hurt, William	21st	Infantry	Co. D
Johnson, Harry	11th	Cavalry	Co. D
Johnson, Samuel	21st	Infantry	Co. C
Johnson, William	21st	Infantry	Co. F
Jones, Amos	6th	Cavalry	Co. E
Jones, George	11th	Cavalry	Co. D
Jones, Jerry	21st	Infantry	Co. A
Kealin, Benjamin	6th	Infantry	Co. H
Lewis, Charles	6th	Infantry	Co. I
Lewis, Samuel	1st	Cavalry	Co. L
Lewis, Samuel	7th	Cavalry	Co. G
Marshall, John	27th	Infantry	Co. H
McBee, Andrew	2nd	Lt. Arty.	
McCarl, Jack	30th	Infantry	Co. G

Name	Regiment	Branch	Company	
McCoy, William	11th	Cavalry	Co. G	
Milam, Joseph	10th	Infantry	Co. H	
Milor, Vesia	21st	Infantry	Co. E	
Mines, Benjamin	6th	Infantry	Co. B	
Moore, Samuel	23rd	Infantry	Co. D	
Oaks, Green	11th	Cavalry	Co. C, M	
Parham, John	6th	Infantry	Co. B	
Parker, Anderson	21st	Infantry	Co. I	
Petre, Alford C.	10th	Infantry	Co. B	
Pickett, Nicholas	10th	Cavalry	Co. E	
Pierson, Henry	10th	Infantry	Co. K	
Poe, John	2nd	St. Mil. Cavalry	Co. K	
Porter, Thomas O.	26th	Infantry	Co. H	
Potilla, Henderson	11th	Cavalry	Co. C	
Potilla, Henderson	3rd	Cavalry	Co. C, B	
Powell, George	1st	Eng.	Co. D, C.	
Powell, George	West Eng. Reg. Vol.			
Price, William	6th	Infantry	Co. C	
Rainy, William	21st	Infantry	Co. D	
Rally, Alfred	1st	Infantry	Co. I	
Ransom, Adam	7th	Infantry	Co. I	
Reed, George	West Eng. Reg. Vol.		Co. C	*
Riggins, Horatio	1st	Infantry	Co. F	
Rooks, Joseph (James)	7th	Cavalry	Co. M	
Ross, Robert	11th	Infantry	Co. G	
Rubin, Roder	7th	Infantry	Co. G	
Runnells, Thomas	21st	Infantry	Co. E	
Ruth, Isaac	8th	St. Mil. Cav.	Co. L	
Ryan, Thomas	35th	Infantry	Co. E	
Sanders, S????	1st	Lt. Arty. Btty.	Co. K	
Saunders, George	23rd	Infantry	Co. K	
Sayers, Joseph	6th	Infantry	Co. G	
Shellant, Ensley	7th	Infantry	Co. H	
Silor, Joseph	1st	Cavalry	Co. M	
Simes, Elijah	6th	Cavalry	Co. H	
Simpson, Amos	11th	Cavalry	Co. F	
Simpson, Frederick	10th	Infantry	Co. F	
Simpson, Julius	11th	Cavalry	Co. F	
Sloan, Ira	11th	Cavalry	Co. B	
Smith, Bailey	10th	Infantry	Co. G	
Smith, Francis	2nd	Lt. Arty. Btty.	Co. C	
Smith, Jack	8th	Infantry	Co. B	
Smith, Pompey	6th	Infantry	Co. G	
Smith, Samuel	3rd	Cavalry	Co. A	
Smith, Samuel	11th	Cavalry	Co. A	

Smith, Wilson 18th Infantry Co. C
Spite, James 21st Infantry Co. B
Stokes, Robert 6th Infantry Co. F
Stubbs, Alexander 10th Infantry Co. G
Tate, Lawrence 6th Infantry Co. D
Taylor, Gabriel 8th Infantry Co. K
Taylor, Isham 24th Infantry Co. E
Taylor, Isham 26th Infantry Co. K
Taylor, John T. 8th Cavalry Co. A
Taylor, Richard 21st Infantry Co. A
Taylor, Thomas 7th St. Mil. Cavalry Co. F
Thadeus, Francis 10th Infantry Co. H
Thiesan, George 6th Infantry Co. A
Thomas, Alexander 26th Infantry Co. A
Thornton, Luke 30th Infantry Co. C
Tichnor, Jacob 2nd Cavalry ?
Tille, Augustus 3rd U.S. Res. Corp Infantry
Titsworth, Willis 24th Infantry Co. I, H
Tittsworth, Willis 21st Infantry Co. C
Tucker, Samuel 8th Infantry Co. H
Tucker, Augustus 15th Infantry Co. K
Twitchell, Felix 11th Cavalry Co. H
Waddlow, Nelson 2nd Lt. Art'y. Btt'y. I
Wadw, ?? 26th Infantry Co. E
Wagdon,, John 21st Infantry Co. A
Walker, Squire 2nd Lt. Art'y. Btt'y. K
Warren, King 10th Infantry Co. A
Warren, King 26th Infantry Co. K
Washington, Dougherty 8th Infantry Co. E
Washington, George 6th Infantry Co. F
Washington, George 8th Infantry Co. I
Washington, George 21st Infantry Co. B
Washington, Thomas 6th Infantry Co. B
Watkins, Bell 18th Infantry Co. B
Watkins, Primus 3rd Cavalry Co. K
Wesley, John 2nd St. Mil. Calvary Co. F
West, James 15th Infantry Co. C
White, Jacob 18th Infantry Co. D
Whitecar, Jacob 6th Infantry Co. B
Whitfield, Henry 10th Cavalry Co. C
Whitfield, Marshall 11th Infantry Co. B
Whiticar, Isaac 18th Infantry Co. E
Whitley, Edward 21st Infantry Co. B
Williams, Henry 10th Infantry Co. H
Williams, Billy 8th Infantry Co. D

Williams, Jesse	18th	Infantry	Co. G
Williams, John	30th	Infantry	Co. F
Williams, Joseph	21st	Infantry	Co. F
Williams, King	18th	Infantry	Co. I
Williams, Perry	6th	Cavalry	Co. G
Williams, Thomas	2nd	Lt. Art'y.	Btt'y. A
Wills, Ireland	11th	Cavalry	Co. E
Winston, Samuel	21st	Infantry	Co. E
Woan, Andy	21st	Infantry	Co. E
Wood, Robert	15th	Infantry	Co. I
Woods, Robert	2nd	Infantry	Co. I
Wright, William	7th	Cavalry	Co. I
York, Hugh (Huell)	23rd	Infantry	Co. A
York, Nelson	23rd	Infantry	Co. B
York, Thomas	23rd	Infantry	Co. B
Young, Moses	21st	Infantry	Co. E
Young, Thomas	21st	Infantry	Co. E

☆NEBRASKA

Johnson, Harrison	1st	Cavalry	Co. H
Smith, Alfred	1st	Cavalry	Co. K

☆NEVADA

Maddox, George	Cavalry 1st Bn.	Co. B
Opelesley, Augustus	Cavalry 1st Bn.	Co. B
Robinson, Joseph R.	Cavalry` 1st Bn.	Co. B
Sharp, William Henry	Infantry 1st Bn.	Co. A
Tasco, William J.	Infantry 1st Bn	Co. C
Wright, John	Cavalry 1st Bn.	Co. D

☆NEW HAMPSHIRE

Africanus, Scipio	2nd	Infantry	Co. G
Africanus, Scipio	12th	Infantry	Co. I
Bisker/Basker, Henry	12th	Infantry	Co. B
Bisker/Basker, Henry	2nd	Infantry	Co. D
Dorsey, Frank	2nd	Infantry	Co. B, F;
Dorsey, Frank	10th	Infantry	Co. G;
Dorsey, Frank	12th	Infantry	Co. D
Dorsey, John H.(a.k.a. William)	2nd	Infantry	Co. B
Dorsey, John H.	12th	Infantry	Co. B

Forrest, Frank	8th	Infantry	Co. C
Gunn, George W.	12th	Infantry	Co. A
Hawkins, Henry	8th	Infantry	Co. C
Lee, Lucius	2nd	Infantry	Co. E
Lee, Lucius	12th	Infantry	Co. C
Medley, Richard	2nd	Infantry	Co. C
Medley, Richard	12th	Infantry	Co. D
Smith, Orin	8th	Infantry	Co. A
Stephenson, Joseph	2nd	Infantry	Co. G
Stephenson, Joseph	12th	Infantry	Co. A
Yerbe, John	12th	Infantry	Co. C
Yerbe, John	2nd	Infantry	Co. E
Young, Willis	8th	Infantry	Co. A

☆NEW JERSEY

Amos, Charles	3rd	Cavalry	Co. C, M
Anders, Joseph H.	3rd	Cavalry	Co. A
Anderson, Thomas	3rd	Cavalry	Co. M
Anderson, William	3rd	Cavalry	Co. L
Brister, Charles	34th	Infantry	Co. A
Coward, Charles	34th	Infantry	Co. A
Daniels, Harrison	2nd	Cavalry	Co. B
Davis, Robert	3rd	Cavalry	Co. G
Davis, William	3rd	Cavalry	Co. B
Fisher, Benjamin	34th	Infantry	Co. H
Forman, William	3rd	Cavalry	Co. L
Glasgow, George	3rd	Cavalry	Co. F
Hagerman, Aaron	3rd	Cavalry	Co. G
Holmes, James H.	34th	Infantry	Co. B
Jackson, Peter	Vet. Infantry 1st Batt'n		Co. B
Jackson, Peter	1st	Infantry	Co. K
Johnson, Henry	3rd	Cavalry	Co. H
Johnson, William	34th	Infantry	Co. E
Lemmon, William	3rd	Cavalry	Co. I
Martin, Mili	34th	Infantry	Co. G
Miller, Peter	3rd	Cavalry	Co. E
Nixon, James	34th	Infantry	Co. B
Oliver, Jeremiah	1st	Infantry	Co. K
Oliver, jerimiah	Vet. Infantry 1st Batt'n		Co. B
Redding, John F.	3rd	Cavalry	Co. G
Rice, William	3rd	Cavalry	Co. B
Robertson, Anthony	1st	Infantry	Co. K
Scott, William	3rd	Cavalry	Co. K
Scudder, Aaron	34th	Infantry	Co. E

Thompson, Francis	3rd	Cavalry	Co. I
Tucker, Charles	34th	Infantry	Co. E, G
Wallace, John	3rd	Cavalry	Co. K
White, Alexander	3rd	Cavalry	Co. M
Wilson, Henry	3rd	Cavalry	Co. M
Wilson, John	34th	Infantry	Co. B, K
Wright, James	3rd	Cavalry	Co. A, I, M

☆**NEW MEXICO** None

☆**NEW YORK**

Abraham, James	91st	Infantry	Co. H
Adams, William	160th	Infantry	Co. K
Adkins, Frederick	91st	Infantry	Co. F, K
Adkins, Peter	133rd	Infantry	Co. F, K
Alfred, John	14th	Cavalry	Co. B
Anderson, Bruce	142nd	Infantry Co. K	Medal of Honor*
Anderson, David	98th	Infantry	Co. F, A
Annon, Alfred	165th	Infantry	Co. A
Baird, Berdant	16th	Heavy Artillery	Co. K
Ball, Edwin	99th	Infantry	Co. K, A
Ball, Edwin	132nd	Infantry	Co. D
Ballard, David	155th	Infantry	Co. E
Barrow, David	133rd	Infantry	Co. A
Batties, John	159th	Infantry	Co. E
Beal, William	162nd	Infantry	Co. A
Beecher, Henry W.	173rd	Infantry	Co. I
Berguin, Morris	176th	Infantry	Co. G
Betts, Samuel	90th	Infantry	Co. K, A
Braide, Alexander	110th	Infantry	Co. K
Briscoe, Emanuel	160th	Infantry	Co. D
Brothers, Tom	155th	Infantry	Co. K
Brown, Abram	91st	Infantry	Co. G
Brown, Abram	159th	Infantry	Co. C
Brown, Adam	159th	Infantry	Co. G
Brown, Amos	156th	Infantry	Co. C
Brown, Bloomfield	51st	Infantry	Co. A
Brown, Bloomfield	109th	Infantry	Co. A
Brown, George	176th	Infantry	Co. E
Brown, James	102nd	Infantry	Co. A
Brown, James	109th	Infantry	Co. D
Brown, John	14th	Cavalry	Co. B
Brown, John	51st	Infantry	Co. C, B
Brown, John	164th	Infantry	Co. F, H

Name	Regiment	Branch	Company
Brown, Richard	91st	Infantry	Co. C
Bryan, Norman	90th	Infantry	Co. A
Bryan, Norman	116th	Infantry	Co. I
Bunck, Henry	178th	Infantry	Co. B
Burnett, John	164th	Infantry	Co. H
Camel, Jackson	128th	Infantry	Co. A
Carey, Edmund	159th	Infantry	Co. D, A
Carr, Edward	99th	Infantry	Co. B
Carr, Edward	132nd	Infantry	Co. I
Carr, Isaac	99th	Infantry	Co. B
Carr, Isaac	132nd	Infantry	Co. A
Chalk, William	155th	Infantry	Co. D
Chew, Henry	51st	Infantry	Co. A
Chew, Henry	109th	Infantry	Co. A
Christian, Watson	96th	Infantry	Co. E
Clavey, John	11th	Cavalry	Co. C
Clay, Henry	178th	Infantry	Co. B
Columbia, Albert	148th	Infantry	Co. B
Conor, Levi	148th	Infantry	Co. B
Cox, George	12th	Cavalry	Co. E
Crandall, Spencer	96th	Infantry	Co. B
Crackman, Patio	81st	Infantry	Co. K
Crow, William	148th	Infantry	Co. B
Davis, King	45th	Infantry	Co. B
Davis, Michael	155th	Infantry	Co. B
Delaney, Henry	90th	Infantry	Co. E
Delaney, Henry	116th	Infantry	Co. A
Diggs, Henry	90th	Infantry	
Dobson, Henry	99th	Infantry	Co. A
Dobson, Henry	132nd	Infantry	Co. D
Dogue, Dennis	91st	Infantry	Co. B
Dougherty, Isaac	156th	Infantry	Co. C
Easer, Charles	99th	Infantry	Co. C
Easton, Henry	182nd	Infantry	Co. C
Eddie, Bob	1st	Engineers	Co. H
Edwards, John	1st	Mtd. Rifles	Co. C
Elic, Frank	159th	Infantry	Co. E
Elliott, Thomas	96th	Infantry	Co. K
Ellis, Hilliard	155th	Infantry	Co. F
Emil, Victor	133rd	Infantry	Co. F
Ennis, Richard	109th	Infantry	Co. C
Epps, James	176th	Infantry	Co. K
Evans, Clem	22nd	Cavalry	Co. H
Fall, George	Lt. Arty.	24th Ind. Battery	
Fletcher, Samuel	174th	Infantry	Co. G

Fox, William	173rd	Infantry	Co. A
Freeman, George E.	14th Hvy.	Artillery	Co. E
Glover, Adam	18th	Cavalry	Co. C, H
Graham, Jefferson	128th	Infantry	Co. D
Graham, Jefferson	144th	Infantry	
Greeley, John	90th	Infantry	Co. F
Greeley, John	116th	Infantry	Co. E
Greeley, Horace	173rd	Infantry	Co. I
Green, James	161st	Infantry	Co. C
Green, Moses	160th	Infantry	Co. I
Green, Samuel	51st	Infantry	Co. I
Griffin, Bald	14th	Cavalry	Co. B
Griffin, Charles P	18th	Cavalry	Co. C
Griffin, George	182nd	Infantry	Co. C
Griffin, George	18th	Infantry	Co. A
Guyan, John	14th Hvy.	Artillery	Co. A
Hall, Benjamin	176th	Infantry	Co. D
Hardy, Tony	Lt. Arty.	8th	Ind. Battery
Hargraves, Joseph	148th	Infantry	Co. A
Harper, Samuel	90th	Infantry	Co. B
Harrison, William H.	90th	Infantry	Co. B
Haywood, Frank	18th	Cavalry	Co. E
Haywood, John	12th	Cavalry	Co. L
Hazen, Samuel	176th	Infantry	Co. I
Henderson, Thomas	182nd	Infantry	Co. I
Henry, William	98th	Infantry	Co. C
Hollin, Humphry	175th	Infantry	Co. A
Hollin, Humphry	99th	Infantry	Co. B
Howard, Jeremiah	108th	Infantry	Co. A
Howard, George	30th	Infantry	Co. D
Hurdel, Wesley	3rd Lt.	Arty. Battery	Co. K
Huzen, Simon	12th	Cavalry	Co. I
Isaac, James	182nd	Infantry	Co. B
Jackson, Aaron	90th	Infantry	Co. C
Jackson, Aaron	133rd	Infantry	Co. K
Jackson, Alexander	156th	Infantry	Co. I
Jackson, Andrew	160th	Infantry	Co. E
Jackson, John H.	175th	Infantry	Co. C
Jackson, Samuel	14th	Infantry	Co. M
James, Frank	18th	Cavalry	Co. C
James, Frank	14th	Cavalry	Co. C
Jefferson, Joseph	165th	Infantry	Co. D
Jefferson, Thomas	155th	Infantry	Co. G
Jefferson, Thomas	164th	Infantry	Co. C
Jenkins, Philip```	160th	Infantry	Co. B

Jenkins, Josiah	173rd	Infantry	Co. E
Johnson, Alec	85th	Infantry	
Johnson, Blunt	176th	Infantry	Co. B
Johnson, Cornelius	182nd	Infantry	Co. C, E
Johnson, Francis	45th	Infantry	Co. F
Johnson, Frederick	162nd	Infantry	Co. H
Johnson, Frederick	174th	Infantry	Co. H
Johnson, Henry	155th	Infantry	Co. C
Johnson, Henry	160th	Infantry	Co. B
Johnson, Israel	91st	Infantry	Co. A
Johnson, Josiah	90th	Infantry	Co. D
Johnson, Lawrence	178th	Infantry	Co. D
Johnson, Richard	14th	Cavalry	Co. A
Johnson, William	178th	Infantry	Co. D
Johnston, John	155th	Infantry	Co. C
Johnston, Overton	160th	Infantry	Co. C
Johnston, Peter	182nd	Infantry	Co. I
Jonas, Aaron	99th	Infantry	Co. A
Jonas, Aaron	132nd	Infantry	Co. G
Jones, Adam	165th	Infantry	Co. A
Jones, Andrew	164th	Infantry	Co. H
Jones, Benjamin	116th	Infantry	Co. G
Jones, Henry	27th	Cavalry	Co. G
Jones, Henry	98th	Infantry	Co. I
Jones, Peter	176th	Infantry	Co. H
Jones, Samuel	161st	Infantry	Co. C
Jones, Scipio	90th	Infantry	Co. E
Jones, Thomas	110th	Infantry	Co. I
Jones, Toney	90th	Infantry	Co. A
Jones, William	178th	Infantry	Co. D
Kerson, Daniel	182nd	Infantry	Co. H
King, Davis	58th	Infantry	Co. B
Knight, Jacob	155th	Infantry	Co. E
Latham, Simon	98th	Infantry	Co. E
Lee, Elisha or Elias	155th	Infantry	Co. I
Leverett, Carolina	1st	Engineers	Co. H
Levi, Antoine	162nd	Infantry	Co. H
Levi, George	109th	Infantry	
Levi, Henry	90th	Infantry	Co. K, A
Lomax, Andrew	14th	Cavalry	Co. M
Long, Benjamin	98th	Infantry	Co. D
Mack, James	161st	Infantry	Co. I
Mackey, Joseph	165th	Infantry	Co. E
Martin, Alexander	155th	Infantry	Co. A
Mashack, Frederick	176th	Infantry	Co. F

Mason, Charles	173rd	Infantry	Co. E
Mason, John	114th	Infantry	Co. C
Matthew, Thomas	51st	Infantry	Co. B
McCoy, John	165th	Infantry	Co B
McLean, Henry	7th	Heavy Artillery	Co. F
Mead, William	18th	Cavalry	Co. I
Meadows, Luke	98th	Infantry	Co. A, B
Miles, Joseph	182nd	Infantry	Co. G
Miller, Charles	91st	Infantry	Co. C
Miller, Edward	159th	Infantry	Co. E
Morgan, Isaac	182nd	Infantry	Co. A
Morgan, William	161st	Infantry	Co. B
Morrell, Paul	165th	Infantry	Co. D
Myers, David	162nd	Infantry	Co. I
Nazree, Thomas	155th	Infantry	Co. B
Neuson, James	155th	Infantry	Co. E
Nickerson, Alexander	90th	Infantry	Co. K
Nixon, Wilson	155th	Infantry	Co. C
Olmstead, Manuel	160th	Infantry	Co. F
Page, George W.	148th	Infantry	Co. E
Perkins, Albert	Lt. Art'y.	26th Ind. Battery	
Perry, Edmund	91st	Infantry	Co. C
Phillips, Spencer	91st	Infantry	Co. H
Pierce, John	18th	Cavalry	Co. D
Prue, William	173rd	Infantry	Co. A
Pugh, Henry	85th	Infantry	Co. C
Rann, Jesse	116th	Infantry	Co. C
Ray, Samuel	11th	Cavalry	Co. I
Reynolds, Ashley	99th	Infantry	Co. B, C
Reynolds, Ashley	137th	Infantry	Co. H
Ritterson, Sam	98th	Infantry	Co. B
Rogers, Henry	182nd	Infantry	Co. K
Rolac/Roulhac, John	85th	Infantry	Co. C
Rowler, Henry	162nd	Infantry	Co. B
Rowler, Henry	174th	Infantry	Co. B
Russell, William	51st	Infantry	Co. H
Sachell, W.	96th	Infantry	Co. A
Savage, James	164th	Infantry	Co. I
Scott, Nathan	162nd	Infantry	Co. C
Shepard, Nelson	Lt. Artillery	24th Ind. Btt'y.	
Shepard, Nelson	3rd	Artillery	Co. L
Sheppard, Jeremiah	99th	Infantry	Co. B
Sheppard, Jerimiah	132nd	Infantry	Co. C
Sidney, Washington	160th	Infantry	Co. I
Simms, Henry	160th	Infantry	Co. C

Simson, James	173rd	Infantry	Co. D
Skater, E.	155th	Infantry	Co. D
Smart, John	160th	Infantry	Co. K
Smith, Frederick	160th	Infantry	Co. D
Snowden, Lewis	51st	Infantry	Co. C
Snowden, Lewis	109th	Infantry	Co. C
Spohn, Ruby	162nd	Infantry	Co. C
Sullivan, George	3rd	Lt. Art'y. Battery	Co. C
Thomas, George	51st	Infantry	Co. C
Thomas, George	160th	Infantry	Co. A
Thomas, George	164th	Infantry	Co. E
Thomas, Tom Henry	133rd	Infantry	Co. I
Thompson, George	165th	Infantry	Co. D
Thompson, John	98th	Infantry	Co. D
Tow, Israel	164th	Infantry	Co. C
Turner, James	99th	Infantry	Co. B
Turner, James	132nd	Infantry	Co. I
Turner, Stephen	91st	Infantry	Co. B
Turner, Washington	162nd	Infantry	Co. E
Walker, George	18th	Cavalry	Co. C
Walker, Green	133rd	Infantry	Co. K
Walker, James	132nd	Infantry	Co. A
Walker, William	22nd	Cavalry	Co. I
Wallace, Charles	173rd	Infantry	Co. F
Washington, George	3rd	Lt. Arty.	Co. L
Washington, George	91st	Infantry	Co. E
Washington, George	159th	Infantry	Co. B
Washington, George	162nd	Infantry	Co. I
Washington, Joseph	165th	Infantry	Co. B
Whitehead, Henry	99th	Infantry	Co. B
Williams, Albert	132nd	Infantry	Co. E
Willis, Pauldo	132nd	Infantry	Co. G
Wood, James	128th	Infantry	Co K

☆ NORTH CAROLINA

Barnett, John	3rd	Mtd. Infantry	Co. B
Braddy, Moses	1st	Infantry	Co. G
Brinkley, Simon	1st	Infantry	Co. F
Brown, Mingo	1st	Infantry	Co. B
Cox, John	1st	Infantry	Co. C
Dowe, Hilliard	1st	Infantry	Co. G
Graham, Torey	1st	Infantry	Co. L
Horton, William R.	3rd	Mtd. Infantry	Co. I
Lewis, Timothy	1st	Infantry	Co. H

Lodge, Charles	1st	Infantry	Co. E
McKee, Willson	3rd	Mtd. Infantry	Co. E
Mitchell, Berry (Bery)	3rd	Mtd. Infantry	Co. B
Moore, Taylor	3rd	Mtd. Infantry	Co. A
Stadon, Randall	1st	Infantry	Co. I
Taylor, James	1st	Infantry	Co. E
Ward, Jerry	1st	Infantry	Co. B
Wells, James	3rd	Mtd. Infantry	Co. B
Williams, Riley	1st	Infantry	Co. A
Wilson, Robert	3rd	Mtd. Infantry	Co. A

☆OHIO

Adams, Henry	46th	Infantry	Co. A
Anderson, George	2nd	Cavalry	Co. G
Andrews, Jerry	32nd	Infantry	Co. E
Anthony, William	106th	Infantry	Co. C
Armstrong, Ed	79th	Infantry	Co. F
Ashby, Joseph	3rd	Cavalry	Co. H
Banks, Simon	74th	Infantry	Co. C
Bell, Enos	26th	Lt. Art'y.	Indpt. Batt'y
Blandon, John	9th	Cavalry	Co. G
Booker, Andrew	32nd	Infantry	Co. H
Booker, Elisha	32nd	Infantry	Co. H
Bradgett, Cagy	71st	Infantry	Co. C
Brown, Samuel	32nd	Infantry	Co. H
Bual, Jackson	32nd	Infantry	Co. G
Buckner, David	2nd	Infantry	Co. G
Burney, Benjamin	32nd	Infantry	Co. F
Carter, John	Union Light Guards	Cavalry	
Clark, Berry	31st	Infantry	Co. H
Clark, Charles	3rd	Calvary	Co. B
Clark, Josiah	31st	Infantry	Co. H
Coleman, Frederick	32nd	Infantry	Co. H
Coleman, Lee	3rd	Cavalry	Co. H
Coleman, Robert	3rd	Cavalry	Co. C
Colwell, Edmund	32nd	Infantry	Co. A
Cordell, Lee	32nd	Infantry	Co. D
Danna, Charles	17th	Infantry	Co. B
David, Doctor	54th	Infantry	Co. A
Dixon, Lock	32nd	Infantry	Co. A
Driggins, Edmund/Edward	98th	Infantry	Co. F
Driggins, Edmund/Edward	74th	Infantry	Co. B
Driggins, Peter	74th	Infantry	Co. K
Garvine, Samuel	17th	Infantry	Co. K

Gay, Freeman	17th	Infantry	Co. C
Hazard, Robert	32nd	Infantry	Co. A
Hemings, Thomas Eston	175th	Infantry	Co. E
Hemings, William Beverly	73rd	Infantry	Co. H
Henderson, Beverly	25th	Infantry	Co. K
Henderson, Beverly	107th	Infantry	Co. D
Henry, William	57th	Infantry	Co. B
Howes, Benjamin	32th	Infantry	Co. G
Hye, Thomas	89th	Infantry	Co. I
Jackson, John	32nd	Infantry	Co. D
Jones, Cato	31st	Infantry	Co. K
Kimbeau, James	57th	Infantry	Co. B
Mason, Joseph	106th	Infantry	Co. C
Mason, Newman	106th	Infantry	Co. D
Maxwell, Daniel	3rd	Cavalry	Co. K
McGrew, Parker	32nd	Infantry	Co. K
McMichael, Isham	32nd	Infantry	Co. H
McMillen, Daniel	Lt. Arty.		10th Ind. Battery
Moore, Anderson	69th	Infantry	Co. E
Moore, Anderson	121st	Infantry	Co. I
Morrow, Alfred	32nd	Infantry	Co. D
Palmer, Benjamin	31st	Infantry	Co. G
Palmer, George	113th	Infantry	Co. A
Palmer, James	31st	Infantry	Co. G
Palmer, James	89th	Infantry	Co. K
Palmer, Moses	89th	Infantry	Co. K
Palmer, Moses	31st	Infantry	Co. I
Palmer, Rufus	31st	Infantry	Co. F
Parker, Jones	31st	Infantry	Co. I
Pointer, David	113th	Infantry	Co. H
Pointer, Pompey	113th	Infantry	Co. H
Pollhill, William	92nd	Infantry	Co. C
Powers, Alfred	32nd	Infantry	Co. F
Rainer, Mark (Mack)	32nd	Infantry	Co. B
Rodgers, Sidney	32nd	Infantry	Co. K
Roundtree, Martin	Lt. Art'y.		5th Ind. Battery
Roundtree, Martin	Lt. Art'y.		11th Ind. Battery
Russell, George W.	32nd	Infantry	Co. A
Scott, Benjamin	32nd	Infantry	Co. F
Simes, Martin	69th	Infantry	Co. K
Simes, Martin	121st	Infantry	Co. K
Smith, William	32nd	Infantry	Co. E
Still, David	63rd	Infantry	Co. C
Strothers, Joshua	32nd	Infantry	Co. E
Thomas, Nathaniel	32nd	Infantry	Co. F

Turk, Josiah	92nd	Infantry	Co. F
Vaughn, Thomas	32nd	Infantry	Co. E
Wadley, Samuel	32nd	Infantry	Co. G
Walker, Isaac	3rd	Cavalry	Co. F
Watson, Madison	32nd	Infantry	Co. G
Williams, George	32nd	Infantry	Co. A
Williams, Sidney	32nd	Infantry	Co. G
Yost, Gabriel	71st	Infantry	Co. G
Young, Jasper	89th	Infantry	Co. K

☆**OREGON** None

☆**PENNSYLVANIA**

Atus, James	57th	Infantry	
Brister, Charles	82nd	Infantry	Co. G
Bullard, Aaron	47th	Infantry	Co. D
Bullard, John	47th	Infantry	Co. D, J
Clark, William	7th	Cavalry	Co. G.
Clemens, Samuel	7th	Cavalry	Co. H
Cloud, Solomon	8th	Infantry	Co. B
Cobb, William	28th	Infantry	Co. B
Fisher, William	15th	Cavalry	Co. H
Cooper, William	7th	Cavalry	Co. I
Day, Alfred	3rd	Cavalry	Co. G
Elick, John	7th	Cavalry	Co. D
Flander, Samuel	55th	Infantry	Co. K
Folk, Thomas	11th	Cavalry	Co. M
Freeman, George	103rd	Infantry	Co. I
Garrett, Dolphus	103rd	Infantry	Co. K
Graham, David	7th	Cavalry	Co. M
Granville, Samuel	103rd	Infantry	Co. B
Hardy (McRae), Titus	103rd	Infantry	Co. K
Hickman, James	7th	Cavalry	Co. C
Holmes, Charles	82nd	Infantry	Co. G
Holmes, Daniel	7th	Cavalry	Co. I
Johnson, Henry	101st	Infantry	Co. C
Jones, James	19th	Cavalry	
Langley, George W.	11th	Cavalry	Co. A
Lee, Edward	7th	Cavalry	Co. L
MacDryfuss, Shelby	7th	Cavalry	Co. F
Mackey, Henry	58th	Infantry	Co. G
Mayfield, John	11th	Cavalry	Co. A
McDonald, Alfred	7th	Cavalry	Co. M
Mercer, Raymond	58th	Infantry	Co. A

Moore, Hamilton	7th	Cavalry	Co. K
Myott, John	101st	Infantry	Co. I
Oakley, Peter	15th	Cavalry	Co. I
Pacien (Patience), Crowder	103rd	Infantry	Co. C
Patton, David	7th	Cavalry	Co. E
Pete, Thomas	28th	Infantry	Co. B
Pigg, Benjamin	15th	Cavalry	Co. C
Rice, David	7th	Cavalry	Co. A
Robinson, Cornelius	1st	Lt. Arty. Battery	Co. E
Robison, Philip	55th	Infantry	Co. H
Robison, Toby	55th	Infantry	Co. H
Rooker, Handy	15th	Cavalry	Co. C
Sanders, Ben	55th	Infantry	Co. K
Small, Napoleon/Nabuka	55th	Infantry	Co. C
Smith, Jonas	58th	Infantry	Co. D
Smith, Joseph	55th	Infantry	Co. B
Smith, Philip	7th	Cavalry	Co. F
Snipe, Abraham	55th	Infantry	Co. C
Snipe, Ishmael	55th	Infantry	Co. C
Stephens, George E.	26th	Infantry	
Stewart, Stephen	7th	Cavalry	Co. K
Suggs, Edward	58th	Infantry	Co. B
Suggs, Henry	58th	Infantry	Co. B
Thomas, John	19th	Cavalry	Co. A
Townson, Randal	7th	Cavalry	Co. E
Vigle, William	3rd	Cavalry	Co. G
West, Richard	103rd	Infantry	Co. I
Wilson, Thomas	3rd	Cavalry	Co. G

☆RHODE ISLAND

Augustus, Alfred	5th	Heavy Artillery	Co. A
Augustus, London	5th	Heavy Artillery	Co. A
Henry, William	5th	Heavy Artillery	Co. K
Lewis, Noah	5th	Heavy Artillery	Co. F
?Teel, Ashleigh	5th	Heavy Artillery	?
?Teel, Edmund	5th	Heavy Artillery	Co. E

☆TENNESSEE

Babbitt, Erastmus	3rd	Cavalry	Co. A
Bailey, Joseph	10th	Infantry	Co. B
Bell, Ellick	3rd	Cavalry	Co. C
?Bell, Richard	3rd	Cavalry	Co. H
Carter, Simon	13th	Cavalry	Co. E

Hall, Caesar	3rd	Mounted Infantry	Co. B
Hours, Merret	13th	Cavalry	?
Murphy, Jones	10th	Infantry	Co. H
Potts, Elbert	10th	Infantry	Co. G
Price, Jackson	3rd	Mounted Infantry	Co. B
Smith, Henderson	5th	Cavalry	Co. B

☆**TEXAS**

Jackson, Andrew	1st	Cavalry	Co. E

☆**VIRGINIA** None

☆**VERMONT**

Brooks, Thomas	8th	Infantry	Co. K
Clay, Henry	8th	Infantry	Co. G
Henry, John	8th	Infantry	Co. G
Smith, William	8th	Infantry	Co. H
Stewart, William	8th	Infantry	Co. I

☆**WEST VIRGINIA**

McMurray, James	9th	Infantry	Co. C
Still, Andrew Jackson	9th	Infantry	Co. C
Still, David	63rd	Infantry	Co. C
Still, George Washington	13th	Infantry	Co. I
Still, Henry	9th	Infantry	Co. F

☆**WISCONSIN**

Alexander, Thomas	4th	Cavalry	Co. H
Alston, Isaac	4th	Cavalry	Co. F
Bailey, Francis	4th	Cavalry	Co. C
Bentley, Benjamin	4th	Cavalry	Co. K
Blue, Archy	4th	Cavalry	Co. G
Brides, Mac	4th	Cavalry	Co. F
Brown, William	4th	Cavalry	Co. A
Bryder, Mac	4th	Cavalry	Co. F
Butler, Joseph	4th	Cavalry	Co. E
Carter, Charles	4th	Cavalry	Co. A
Cate, Nicholas	4th	Cavalry	Co. C

Clark, John	4th	Cavalry	Co. A
Clifton, Lindsey	4th	Cavalry	Co. K
Dodget, Archibald	4th	Cavalry	Co. E,
Doyle, Alex	4th	Cavalry	Co. F
Emmet, Robert	4th	Cavalry	Co. K
Frances, Peter	4th	Cavalry	Co. D
Gale, Sam	4th	Cavalry	Co. G
Gayton, Peter	4th	Cavalry	Co. G
Germany, John	4th	Cavalry	Co. G
Graham, Antoine	4th	Cavalry	Co. E
Holmes, Daniel	4th	Cavalry	Co. A,
Jefferson, Beverly (Hemings)	1st	Infantry	Co. E
Jefferson, John Wayles (Hemings)	8th	Infantry	Colonel
Jefferson, Thomas	4th	Cavalry	Co. H
Johnson, Spencer	4th	Cavalry	Co. H
Johnson, Spenser	4th	Cavalry	Co. H
Jones, Spencer	4th	Cavalry	Co. A
Kelly, William	4th	Cavalry	Co. C
Laterfield (Satterfield), Louis	4th	Cavalry	Co. B
Leonard, Sam	4th	Cavalry	Co. G
Mack, James	4th	Cavalry	Co. L
McDade, James	4th	Cavalry	Co. F
Moore, Frank	4th	Cavalry	Co. E
Muck, James	4th	Cavalry	Co. L
Perry, Commodore	4th	Cavalry	Co. G
Seymore, Antoine	4th	Cavalry	Co. I
Smith, Isaac	4th	Cavalry	Co. C
Smith, Thomas	4th	Cavalry	Co. I
Strange, Isaac	4th	Cavalry	Co. E
Thomas, Edmund	4th	Cavalry	Co. I
Thomas, John	4th	Cavalry	Co. C
Thompson, Moses	4th	Cavalry	Co. F
Trempleau, Thomas	4th	Cavalry	Co. H
Trempleau, Joseph	4th	Cavalry	Co. H
Walker, Henry	4th	Cavalry	Co. B
Watson, Frederick	4th	Cavalry	Co. E
While, Thomas W.	4th	Cavalry	Co. L
White, Wilson	4th	Cavalry	Co. D
Williams, Albert	4th	Cavalry	Co. D

THE NATIONAL CIVIL WAR MUSEUM

Respectfully Honors
The
Memory
And
Military Service
Of

CROWDER PACIEN
CO C 103RD REGT
PA VOL INF US

During the American Civil War, 1861 - 1865. In recognition of his selfless devotion to duty, this Veteran's personal service is commemorated on The Walk of Valor, at The National Civil War Museum, Harrisburg, Pennsylvania.

Recognized on this day of December 15, 2000

George E. Hicks
GEORGE E. HICKS, Chief Executive Officer

American Civil War Museum's Brick

FINAL RESTING PLACES

Allensworth, Allen Lieutenant- Colonel 44th Illinois Infantry	Angelus-Rosedale Cemetery Los Angeles, California
*Anderson, Pvt. Bruce 142nd N.Y. infantry	Green Hill Cemetery Amsterdam, New York
Fox, Pvt. William Dudley 2nd Michigan Cavalry	Highland Cemetery Ypsilanti, Michigan
Graffell, Pvt. Charles 2nd California Cavalry	Oak Hill Cemetery Red Bluffs, California
Guy, Pvt. Benjamin F. 16th Michigan Infantry	W. Wheatland Cemetery Mecosta, Michigan
Lett, Pvt. Aquilla 13th Michigan Infantry	Arlington Cemetery Van Buren Co., Michigan
McKinney, Pvt. Amos 1st Alabama Cavalry	Sykes Cemetery Morgan County, Alabama
Patience, Pvt. Crowder 103rd Penna. Infantry	West Pittston Cemetery West Pittston, Pennsylvania
Pool, Pvt. Thomas 1st Alabama Cavalry	Corinth National Cemetery Corinth, Mississippi
Rolac (Roulhac), Pvt. John 85th N.Y. Infantry	Andersonville Prison Grave 9549
West, Pvt. Simon Samuel 1st Alabama Cavalry	Highland Park Cemetery Warrenville, Ohio

Tombstone of Crowder Patience
West Pittston Cemetery, West Pittston, Pennsylvania

END NOTES

1. U.S. Bureau of the Census, Bicentennial Edition, "Historical Statistics of the United States, Colonial Times to 1979," part 2, p. 1142.
2. Geoffrey C. Ward with Richard and Ken Burns, *The Civil War: An Illustrated History*, (New York: Alfred A. Knopf, Inc. 1990), p. 2.
3. John Hope Franklin., *From Slavery to Freedom: A History of African Americans,* 4th Edition, (New York: Alfred A. Knopf., 1947), p. 215.
4. *Ibid.* p. 216.
5. John McPherson, *Battle Cry of Freedom: The Civil War Era,* (New York: Ballantine Books, 1998), p. 354.
6. Dudley Taylor Cornish, *The Sable Arm: Negro Troops in the Union Army, 1861-1865,* (N.Y.: W.W. Norton & Co., Inc., 1966), Foreword.
7. McPherson, p. 354.
8. Franklin, p. 216.
9. *War of the Rebellion: Official Records of the Union and Confederate Armies.*
10. Cornish.
11. Bennie J. McRae, Jr., "First Kansas Colored Infantry Regiment: First Black Unit to Engage the Confederacy," LWF Publishers, reprinted for July 1994 edition *Lest We Forget.*
12. McPherson, p. 499.
13. Franklin, p. 222.
14. Christopher Breiseth, "Lincoln and Frederick Douglass: Another Debate," *Journal of the Illinois State Historical Society*, Vol. LXVIII, No. 1, February 1975, pp. 9-26.
15. McRae.
16. Patricia Click, *Time Full of Trial: The Roanoke Island Freedmen's Colony 1862-1867,* (The University of North Carolina Press, 2001), pp. 55-71.
17. Fort Raleigh National Historic Site, The Freedmen's Colony on Roanoke Island.
18. Click, p. 55.
19. Breiseth.

20. Benjamin Quarles, The Negro in the Civil War, (New York: Da Capo Press, 1953), p. 184.
21. Edwin S. Redkey. *A Grand Army of Black Men*, (Cambridge: Cambridge University Press, 1992), p. 6.
22. *War of the Rebellion: Official Records of the Union and Confederate Armies.*
23. Redkey, p. 6.
24. Thomas Patience pension records in author's possession.
25. John Hope Franklin and Alfred A. Moss, Jr., *From Slavery to Freedom: A History of African Americans*, Seventh Edition, (New York: McGraw-Hill, Inc., 1994), p. 214.
26. Allen Nevins. *The War For the Union, Vo. II: War Becomes Revolution,* (New York: Charles Scribner's Sons 1960) p. 524.
27. Frederick Phisterer, *Statistical Record of the Armies of the United States*, (New York: The Blue and The Gray Press, 1883).
28. Redkey, Introduction, p. 3.
29. James McPherson. *The Negro's Civil War: How American Negroes Felt and Acted During the War For the Union,* (N.Y.: Pantheon Books, 1965), p. 223.
30. The editors of "American Heritage, the Magazine of History," Editor in Charge Richard M. Ketchum, Narrative by Brace (Catlon, N.Y.: American Heritage Publishing Co., Inc., 1960), p. 419.
31. *The Negro in the Civil War*, Eastern Acorn Press with permission of the original publisher, (Harrisburg, Penna,: Historian Times, Inc., 1988), p. 39.
32. Joseph T. Glatthar, *Forged in Battle: The Civil War Alliance of Black Soldiers and White Officers,* (N.Y.: The Free Press, 1990), Preface and Acknowledgement.
33. Franklin and Moss, p. 214.
34. Dudley Taylor Cornish, *The Sable Arm: Negro Troops in the Union Army, 1861-1865*, (N.Y.:W.W. Norton & Co., Inc., 1966), Foreword. The Bureau for Colored Troops, headed by Major Charles W. Foster, was located at No. 551 -17th Street in Washington, D.C.
35. *The Washington Afro-American*, July 11-1998-July 17, 1998, p. A3.
36. Ed Hamilton has also created a sculpture of Booker T. Washington on the campus of Hampton University; Joe Louis'

fist in Detroit, Michigan; the Amistad Memorial in New Haven, Conn.; and others..

37. African American Civil War Museum, Washington, D.C.
38. Civil War Soldier's System (CWSS) at the National Archives, Washington, D.C.
39. *The Roster of Union Soldiers 1861-1865*, a printed copy of the index to the Compiled military Service Records (CMSR), (Wilmington, N.C.:Broadfoot Publishing, 1998).
40. William Gladstone's letter to the editor, "Civil War Times," January 2005. He spent a lifetime collecting documents, images, and three dimensional objects relating to the black experience. His collection was sold to the Pamplin Historical Park in Richmond, Virginia.
41. *War of the Rebellion: Official Records of the Union and Confederate Armies* at the National Archives.
42. Constitution, Article 1, Section 2, until the 14th Amendment.
43. Enlistment record of Crowder Pacien, 1 January 1864.
44. Franklin, p. 231.
45. William Henry Johnson, *Autobiography of Dr. William H. Johnson,* (N.Y.: Haskell House Publishers, 1900), p. 17.
46. *Ibid.* pp. 53-54.
47. Johnson, p. 46. The "Fifth" he noted was the 54th Massachusetts Colored Infantry led by Col. Robert Gould Shaw.
48. William Henry Johnson, *Pine and Palm*, 23 November 1861. The *Pine and Palm* was a Boston publication advocating emigration and colonization of blacks to such places as Haiti.
49. Redkey, p. 355.
50. *Douglass' Monthly*, February 1863, p. 9.
51. Excerpts by Bennie McRae from "An Officer and a Gentleman: Chaplain Allen Allensworth of the Twenty-Fourth Infantry," by William J. Hourihan, Ph.D, Chaplain Branch Historian, *U.S. Army Chaplain Museum Association Newsletter*, July 1989.
52. "Schuykill County Historical Society," Vol. 7, No. 3, 1961. The Pennsylvania companies were the National Light Infantry of Pottsville, the Washington Artillerists of Pottsville, the Ringgold Light Artillery of Reading, the Logan Guard of

Lewistown, and the Allen Infantry of Allentown.

53. Redkey, p. 355
54. War *of the Rebellion: Official Records of the Union and Confederate Armies.*
55. Papers filed at War College at Carlisle Barracks, Carlisle, Pennsylvania.
56. The G.A.R. stanchion is a pole holding a five pointed star symbolizing the five branches of the Army (heavy and light artillery, cavalry, infantry, engineers). It is planted beside the tombstone of a Civil War veteran who had been a member of the fraternal organization. The G.A.R. motto is "Fraternity, Charity, and Loyalty."
57. Article from *Pittston Gazette* 1928; in author's possession.
58. "Pacien" on the discharge record spelled as the recruiter heard it pronounced since Crowder was illiterate.
59. Thomas Patience's pension records.
60. *Pittston Gazette* 1928.
61. Roster of the 103rd Pennsylvania Volunteer Regiment, http://members.aol.com/EvanSlaug/103rd.html
62. Courtesy of Debra Miller Felice, 101st Pennsylvania Volunteers historian.
63. Luther Dickey, *History of the 103rd Regiment: Pennsylvania Veterans, Volunteer Infantry 1861-1865*, (Chicago: L. S., Dickey 1910), p. 84.
64. Cousins Jesse and Isaac Carpenter were successful Exeter, Penna., farmers involved with the Underground Railroad.
65. Crowder Patience's death certificate in possession of author.
66. Letter from the National Civil War Museum, Harrisburg, Pa., George Hicks, Chief Executive Officer, 13 December 2000.
67. Juanita Patience Moss, *Battle of Plymouth, N.C., April 17-20, 1864: The Last Confederate Victory*, (Westminster, Maryland: Willow Bend Books, 2003), p. 176.
68. Dickey, p. 51.
69. Weymouth Jordan and Gerald Thomas, "Massacre at Plymouth," *The North Carolina Historical Review*, Vol. LXXII, No. 2, April 1995, p. 155.
70. Dickey, p. 392.
71. *Ibid.* p. 367.
72. *Ibid.* p. 392.

73. Courtesy of Harry Thompson, curator of the Port O' Plymouth Museum, Plymouth, N.C.
74. Jordan and Thomas, p. 155.
75. *Ibid.*
76. *Ibid.*
77. *Ibid.*
78. *Ibid.*
79. *Records of the 24th Independent Battery, N.Y. Light Artillery, U.S. V.*, compiled by J. W. Merrill, published for the Ladies' Cemetery Association of Perry, N.Y., 1870, p. 119.
80. Courtesy of Alan Marsh, Cultural Curator Specialist, Andersonville Historic Prison Site, Andersonville, Georgia.
81. Official Records (Army), ser. 2, 7:78.
82. Military Barracks in Carlisle, Pa.
83. Samuel Bates, *History of the Pennsylvania Volunteers, 1861-65,* (Harrisburg, Pa.: Singerly, State Printer, Vol. 3, 1869-1871).
84. National Archives Research Room, Washington, D.C.
85. Peggy Sawyer-Williams received the Genealogist of the Year Award for 2006 from the Library of Michigan, Lansing, Michigan. She is the immediate past president of the Fred Hart Williams Genealogical Society in Detroit, Michigan, and a member of Tent # 3 of the Daughters of Union Veterans.
86. Information researched by his great daughter, the late Vivian Fox Porche and his great great granddaughter, Maia Porche.
87. Listed as a mulatto in 1860 and 1880 censuses; courtesty of Peggy Sawyer-Williams.
88. Information given to author in 1998 by the late Fred Crenshaw.
89. en.wikepedia.org/wiki/John_Wayles_Jefferson
90. *Ibid.*
91. *Ibid.*
92. Wisconsin Historical Society.
93. *Scioto Gazette*, Chillicothe, Ohio, 1902.
94. Report of the Research Commission on Thomas Jefferson and Sally Hemings, Thomas Jefferson Foundation, January 2000.
95. National Archives Research Room.
96. Broadfoot.
97. Ancestry.com

98. Broadfoot.
99. Glenda McWhither Todd is the regimental historian of the 1st Alabama Cavalry. She is the author of *First Alabama Cavalry, USA: Homage to Patriotism.*
100. Broadfoot.
101. Quarles, p. 213.
102. Gerald W. Thomas, *Bertie in Blue: Experiences of Bertie County's Union Servicemen During the Civil War*, (Plymouth, N.C.: Beacon Printing, Inc., 1998), p. 4. These white "Buffaloes" are not to be confused with the black "Buffalo Soldiers" after the Civil War.
103. Judkin Jay Browning, *Historical Review*, Vol. LXXVII, No. 3, July 2000.
104. Information courtesy of Glenda McWhirter Todd.
105. Bennie McCrae, historian and website creator of "Lest We Forget" Communications, Trotwood, Ohio.
106. Information courtesy of Glenda McWhirter Todd. Copied from pension records filed by Amos and Malissa McKinney
107. *Ibid.*
108. *Ibid.*
109. Richard's West's pension application.
110. Information courtesy of Glenda Todd.
111. *Ibid.*
112. Telephone conversation with reenactor Frederick Smith on 20 June 2008.
113. Information courtesy of Glenda Todd.
114. http://www1stalabamacavalryvsv.com/

* Medal of Honor recipient Private Bruce Anderson was a member of the 142nd N. Y. Infantry. At the Second Battle of Fort Fisher, N.C., he volunteered with twelve others to advance ahead of the main attack and then successfully cut down the palisade blocking their path. However, because the pertinent military papers were misplaced, he did not receive his award until hiring a lawyer in 1914. Only four of the thirteen soldiers ever received the Medal of Honor, even though all had been recommended by General Adelbert Ames.

Information courtesy of Joseph Mazur

SOURCES

African American Perspectives: Pamphlets from the Daniel A. P. Murray Collection, 1818-1907.

Bartlett, Captain A.W. *History of the 12th Regiment New Hampshire Volunteers in the War of the Rebellion.* Concord, N.H.: Ira C. Evans, 1897.

Bates, Samuel P. *History of Pennsylvania Volunteers, 1861-65.* Harrisburg, Pa.: B. Singerly, State Printer, Vol. 3, 1886-1871.

Bennett, Lerone. "Thomas Jefferson's Negro Grandchildren," *Ebony*, November 1954.

Civil War General News. September 1988.

Click, Patricia. *Time Full of Trial: The Roanoke Island Freedmen's Colony 1862-1867.* The University of North Carolina Press, 2001.

Compiled Service Records of Union Soldiers Who Served in Organizations from the State of Pennsylvania, Record Group 94.

Cornish, Douglas Taylor. *The Sable Arm: Negro Troops in the Union Army, 1861-1865.* New York: W. W. Norton & Co., Inc., 1966.

Dickey, Luther S. *History of the 103rd Regiment: Pennsylvania Veteran Volunteer Infantry 1861-1865.* Chicago, Illinois: L. S. Dickey, 1910.

Franklin, John Hope and Moss, Alfred A. *From Slavery to Freedom: A History of African Americans.* 7th Edition, New York: McGraw-Hill, Inc., 1994.

Franklin, John Hope and Schweninger, Loren. *Runaway Slaves: Rebels on the Plantation.* New York, N.Y: Oxford University Press, 1999.

Gladstone, William, *United States Colored Troops: 1863-1867,* Gettysburg, Pa.: Thomas publications, 1990.

Green, Robert Ewell. *Black Defenders of America 1775-1973.* Chicago: Johnson Publishing Co., Inc., 1974.

Hays, E. Z. *History of the 32nd Regiment: Ohio Veteran Volunteer Infantry*. Columbus, Ohio: Cott & Evans Printers, 1896.

Hays, Martin A. *A History of the 2nd Regiment New Hampshire Volunteers in the War of the Rebellion.* Lakeport, N.H., 1896.

Hurmense, Belinda, *My Folks Don't Want Me to Talk About Slavery,"* Winston-Salem, N.C.: John F. Blair, 1984.

Johnson, William Henry. *Autobiography of Dr. William Henry Johnson.* New York: Haskell House, reprint of 1900 edition, 1970.

Jordan, Weymouth and Thomas, Gerald. "Massacre at Plymouth." *The North Carolina Historical Review.* Vol. LXXII, April 1995.

Journal of the Afro-American Historical and Genealogical Society (AAHGS), Vol. 23, No. 2, Fall 2004.

Mc Pherson, James M. *Battle Cry for Freedom: The Civil War Era.* New York: Oxford University Press, 1998.

______. *The Negro's Civil War.* New York: Ballantine Books, 1965.

Moss, Juanita Patience. *Battle of Plymouth, N.C., April 17-20, 1864: The Last Confederate Victory.* Westminster, Maryland: Willow Bend Books, 2003.

Nevins, Allen. *The War for the Union, Vol. II: War Becomes Revolution.* New York: Charles Scribner's Sons, 1960.

Pension Case Files of Bureau of Pensions and Veterans Administration, 1861-1942.

Phisterer, Frederick. *Statistical Record of the Armies of the United States,* New York, The Gray Press, 1888.

Pittston Gazette. 1928 article about Crowder Pacien, 103rd Pennsylvania Volunteers, Company C.

Port-O-Plymouth Museum, Plymouth, N.C. files of Private Richard West, 103rd Pennsylvania Volunteers, Company I.

Quarles, Benjamin. *The Negro in the Civil War*, New York: Da Capo Press, 1953.

Redkey, Edwin S. *A Grand Army of Black Men.* Cambridge: Cambridge University Press, 1992.

The Roster of Union Soldiers 1861-65. Wilmington, N.C.: Broadfoot Publishers, 1998.

The Shaw Memorial: A Celebration of an American Masterpiece, published by Eastern Press/The Saint-Gaudens National Historic Site, 2002.

The War of the Rebellion: A Compilation of the Official Records of the Union and Confederate Armies, 128 volumes, Washington, D.C.: Government Printing Office, 1880-1891.

Thomas, Gerald W. *Bertie in Blue: Experiences of Bertie County's Union Servicemen During the Civil War.* Plymouth, N.C.: Beacon Printing, Inc., 1998.

War College at Carlisle Barracks, Pennsylvania for files of Private Charles Graffell, 2nd California Cavalry, Company H.

ELECTRONIC SOURCES

Ancestry.com

Bennie J. McRae, Jr. *Lest We Forget.* http://www.lwfaam.net/cw/

Photos of Dedication of Simon West's Tombstone http://www.lwfaam.net/event/highland_park.htm

Roster of the 103rd Pennsylvania Volunteer Regiment. http://members.aol.com/EvanSlaug/103rd.html

The American Civil War Research Database. http://www.alexanderstreet.com

Underground Railroad Workshop: Key People, "William Henry Johnson." http://www.ugrworkshop.com/wjohnson.htm

Wikipedia Encyclopedia en.wikipedia.org/wiki/john_Wayles_Jefferson

Act of May 11, 1912.

No. 1,140,513 Reissue

UNITED STATES OF AMERICA

DEPARTMENT OF THE INTERIOR

BUREAU OF PENSIONS

It is hereby certified That in conformity with the laws of the United States Crowder Patient who was a Private Co. C. 103rd Regiment Pennsylvania Infantry is entitled to a pension at the rate of Sixteen dollars per month, to commence June 6, 1912 and Twenty dollars per month from December 25, 1913 and Twenty-four dollars per month from December 25, 1918.

Given at the Department of the Interior this twenty-sixth day of March one thousand nine hundred and thirteen and of the Independence of the United States of America the one hundred and thirty-seventh

Secretary of the Interior

Countersigned

Commissioner of Pensions

Crowder Patience's Pension Record

INDEX

IN REPLY REFER TO:

United States Department of the Interior

National Park Service
Andersonville National Historic Site
496 Cemetery Road
Andersonville, Georgia 31711
(229) 924-0343

K14(ANDE)

January 13, 2005

Juanita Patience Moss
7801 Colonial Springs Blvd.
Alexandria, VA 22306

Dear Ms Moss:

Andersonville National Historic Site is indeed a place that leaves a lasting impression on many people. People such as you who have a personal connection to the Andersonville story leave a lasting impression on the park staff.

I have enclosed a copy of the materials in the file of Private John Rolac. He was a private in the 85th New York Infantry. He died at Andersonville on September 23, 1864, and is buried in grave 9549. The information in the file is probably the same as the Archives. If you would like a picture of the gravestone, please let me know.

The National Park Service personnel at Andersonville are glad to be of assistance to you.

Sincerely yours,

Don

Don Pettijohn
Park Ranger

From Andersonville National Historic Site

CREATED TO BE FREE

by

Juanita Patience Moss

ISBN: I-58549-704-5

This historical novel is based on the life of an 18-year old runaway slave who joined the 103rd Pennsylvania Regiment when it was garrisoned in Plymouth, N.C. The reason for writing the book was because several historians had told the author there had been no black men serving in white regiments during the Civil War. Juanita Patience Moss knew differently because her great grandfather had been one.

Her research to discover other such men led her to write about her ancestor's 83-year life journey from the sweet potato fields of N.C. to the anthracite coal fields of northeastern Pennsylvania. Escaping from Chowan County, the slave boy Toby became the free man Crowder Pacien (Patience).

Through the letters of a fictitious "Plymouth Pilgrim," the story of the Battle of Plymouth is told. A particularly poignant passage deals with what happened to two captured "Buffaloes" who were brothers.

Readers interested in the coal mining industry will want to read about the plight of seven and eight year-olds who were "breaker boys" working ten hour days, six days a week. The coal mining industry had created another kind of slave.

This book is about one American family, in some ways different from all others but in many ways mirroring many others because it is a story of tenacity and survival. There is something in this book for everyone, regardless of ethnicity.

BATTLE OF PLYMOUTH, N.C.: APRIL 17-20, 1864
THE LAST CONFEDERATE VICTORY
by
JUANITA PATIENCE MOSS
ISBN 1-58549-852-1

Many people have not heard about the Battle of Plymouth, even avid Civil War buffs. Well, that's not surprising because very little has been written about it. Read this detailed and carefully researched book to learn about the second largest battle in North Carolina.

Intense drama took place during four days filled with surprise, fate, intrigue, bravery, ingenuity, hope, daring, dedication, gallantry, victory for the Rebels and disappointment and defeat for the Yankees.

Here eleven black men were serving in white regiments. These and others like them have been forgotten by historians. This book proves to modern nay-sayers that there were some black soldiers in white regiments during the Civil War, the author's ancestor being one of them.

*Have you heard of the **CSS Albemarle**, a ship built not a shipyard as expected, but in a cornfield?*

Are you aware of who is credited with having achieved the most daring venture in all of the Civil War, and that it happened at Plymouth, N.C.?

Even if you do know the answers to all of these questions, you will want to read still more about them in this informative, enlightening and interesting non-fiction book.

ANTHRACITE COAL ART BY CHARLES EDGAR PATIENCE

by

JUANITA PATIENCE MOSS

ISBN 0 -7884-4263-5

Charles Edgar Patience, the grandson of the runaway slave Crowder Patience, who became a Union veteran, was an African American anthracite coal sculptor in northeastern Pennsylvania. Having been taught the skills of coal carving by his father who once had been a breaker boy at a local colliery and later a successful entrepreneur, Edgar took the art to a higher level and fulfilled his aspirations of becoming a recognized sculptor.

His unique work was described in March 1970 issue of **Ebony** *magazine as "the world's most unique sculptor." In 1972 he was listed in* **Who's Who in America.** *Unfortunately, just as his star was rising, he died from the curse of miners, black lung disease. Even though he had never been a miner, the coal dust he had been inhaling throughout his sixty-five years damaged his lungs.*

This book has been written by his daughter for those readers who are old enough to remember when "anthracite was king" in northeastern Pennsylvania and for those who are not old enough to know. It is written for those who have no idea that coal can be a medium for sculpturing. It is written so that both present and future generations may come to know and appreciate the work of the pioneer anthracite coal sculptor, Charles Edgar Patience, who brought forth beauty and universal definition from the Pennsylvania "black diamond." A wealth of photographs and a full name plus subject index enhance the text.

ABOUT THE AUTHOR

JUANITA PATIENCE MOSS, born in northeastern Pennsylvania, graduated from the West Pittston public school system; attended Bennett College in Greensboro, North Carolina; received a B.S. degree from Wilkes College, Wilkes Barre, Pennsylvania; and a M.A. from Farleigh Dickinson University, Rutherford, New Jersey. A retired New Jersey high school biology teacher, she recently has developed an interest in genealogy that led to her researching Union black soldiers whose service in white regiments has not been documented. Her great grandfather, Crowder Patience, who served in the 103rd Pennsylvania Volunteers, was one on them.